A-Z NORTHERN ENGLAND

C000258783

Key to Map Pages	2-3
Road Maps	4-55

Town Plans	
Index to To	

REFERENCE

Motorway	**M1**
Under Construction	
Proposed	
Motorway Junctions with Numbers	
Unlimited Interchange **6** Limited Interchange **7**	
Motorway Service Area (with fuel station) **WOODALL**	Ⓢ
with access from one carriageway only	Ⓢ
Major Road Service Areas (with fuel station) **SWANWICK**	
with 24 hour Facilities	Ⓢ
Primary Route (with junction number) **A55**	
Primary Route Destination	**RIPON**
Dual Carriageways (A & B Roads)	
Class A Road	A675
Class B Road	B5248
Major Roads Under Construction	
Major Roads Proposed	
Fuel Station	
Gradient 1:5(20%) & Steeper (Ascent in direction of arrow)	≪
Toll	*Toll*
Milage between Markers	8
Railway and Station	
Level Crossing and Tunnel	
River or Canal	
County or Unitary Authority Boundary	
National Boundary	+ + + +
Built-up Area	
Village or Hamlet	
Wooded Area	
Spot Height in Feet	• *813*
Relief Above 400' (122m)	
National Grd Reference (Kilometres)	¹00
Area Covered by Town Plan	**SEE PAGE 60**

TOURIST INFORMATION

Airport	✈
Airfield	+
Heliport	
Battle Site and Date	*1066* ⚔
Castle (open to public)	
Castle with Garden (open to public)	
Cathedral, Abbey, church, Friary, Priory	✝
Country Park	
Ferry (vehicular)	
(foot only)	
Garden (open to public)	✳
Golf Course 9 Hole 18 Hole	
Historic Building (open to public)	
Historic Building with Garden (open to public)	
Horse Racecourse	
Lighthouse	
Motor Racing Circuit	
Museum, Art Gallery	
National Park	
National Trust Property (open)	*NT*
(Restricted Opening)	*NT*
Nature Reserve or Bird Sanctuary	
Nature Trail or Forest Walk	
Place of Interest	*Monument* •
Picnic Site	
Railway, Steam or Narrow Gauge	
Theme Park	
Tourist Information Centre	ℹ
Viewpoint (360 degrees)	
(180 degrees)	
Visitor Information Centre	**V**
Wildlife Park	
Windmill	
Zoo or Safari Park	

SCALE

0 1 2 3 4 5 6 7 8 9 Miles

0 1 2 3 4 5 6 7 8 9 10 11 12 13 14 Kilometres

Map Page 4-55   1:221,760
3.5 Miles to 1 inch

EDITION 5   2022

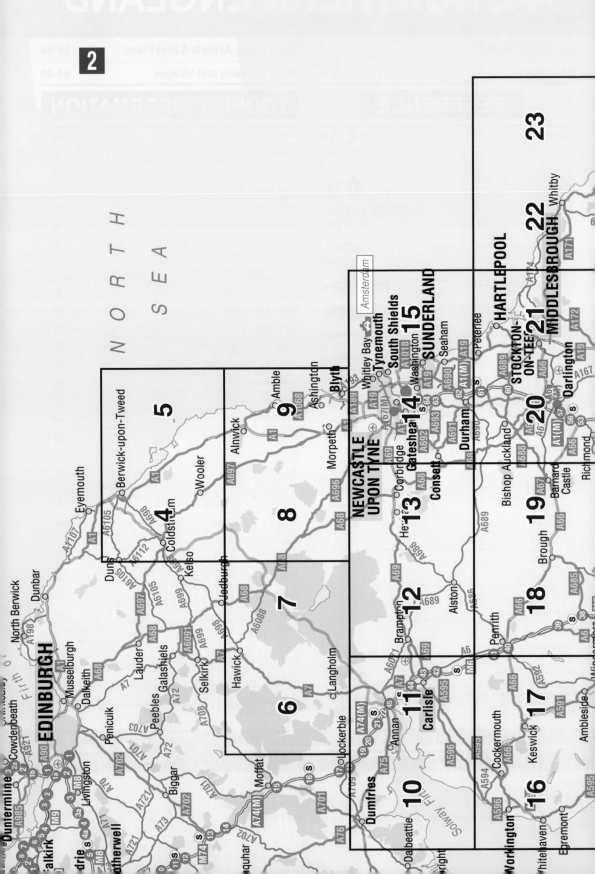

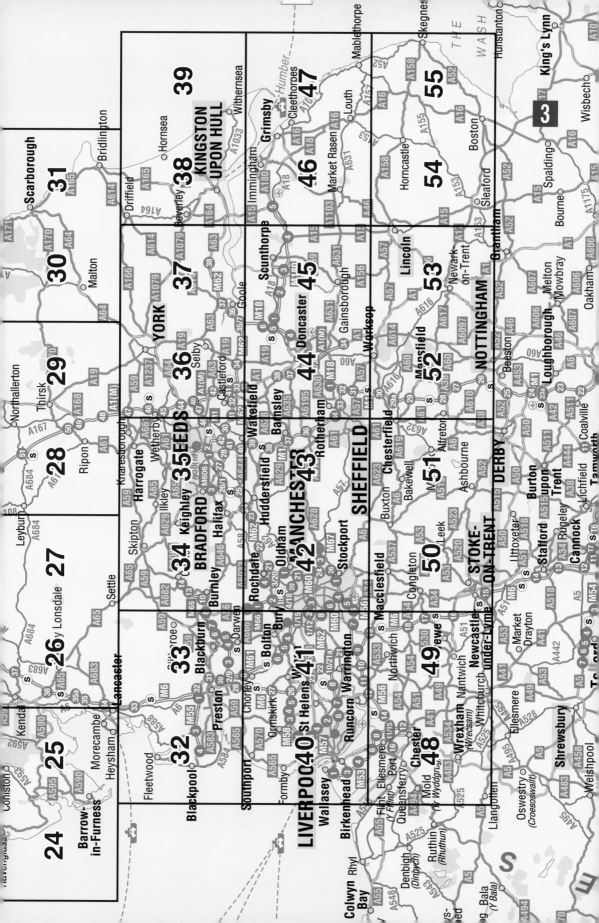

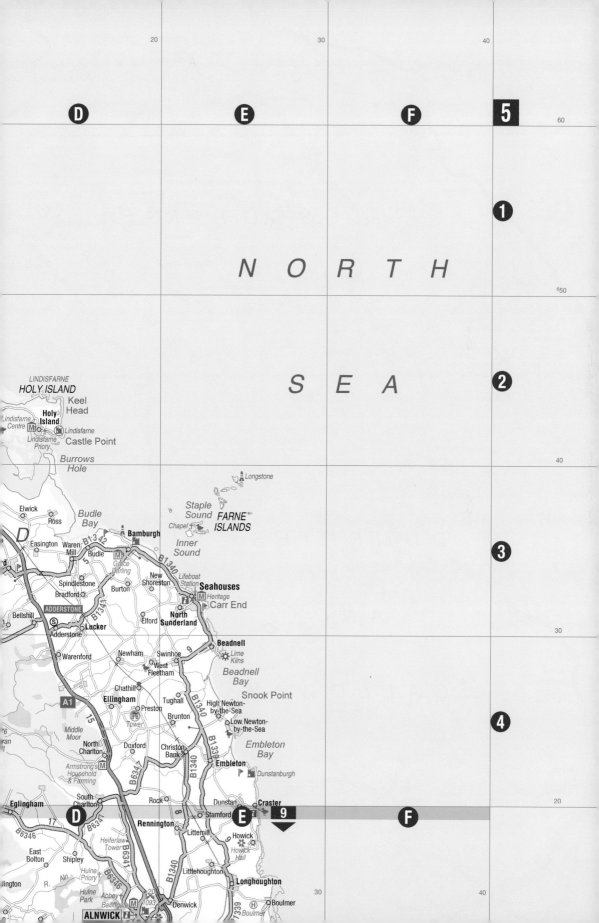

20 **30** **40** 60

D E F **5**

1

N O R T H ⁶50

S E A **2**

40

LINDISFARNE
HOLY ISLAND Keel
Head
Holy
Lindisfarne **Island**
Centre Ⓜ Lindisfarne
Lindisfarne Castle Point
Priory

Burrows
Hole

Elwick *Longstone*
Ross **3**
Budle Staple
Elwick *Bay* Sound FARNE
Ⓓ **Bamburgh** Chapel ISLANDS
Easington Waren B1342 *Inner*
Mill Budle *Sound*
Spindlestone Ⓜ Grace Lifeboat
Darling New Station
Shoreston **Seahouses**
Bradford Burton Ⓜ Heritage 30
ADDERSTONE Elford **North** ⓘ Carr End
Ⓢ Lucker **Sunderland**
Bellshill Adderstone **Beadnell**
Warenford Newham Swinhoe 9 *Lime*
West *Kilns*
Fleetham *Beadnell*
Chathill Tughall *Bay*
Ⓐ1 **Ellingham** Preston *Snook Point* **4**
Brunton High Newton-
Tower by-the-Sea
Middle Doxford Low Newton-
Moor Christon by-the-Sea
North Bank *Embleton* 20
Charlton **Embleton** *Bay*
Armstrong's Ⓜ Dunstanburgh
Household
& Farming Rock Dunstan **Craster**
Eglingham South Stamford Ⓔ **9** F
Charlton Howick
Ⓓ B6341 Rennington Littlemill Howick
Heiferlaw Hall
Tower
East B6346 Littlehoughton **Longhoughton**
Bolton Shipley Hulne
Priory Denwick Ⓗ Boulmer
R. Aln Hulne
Park Abbey
Bailiffgate Ⓜ
ALNWICK 30 40

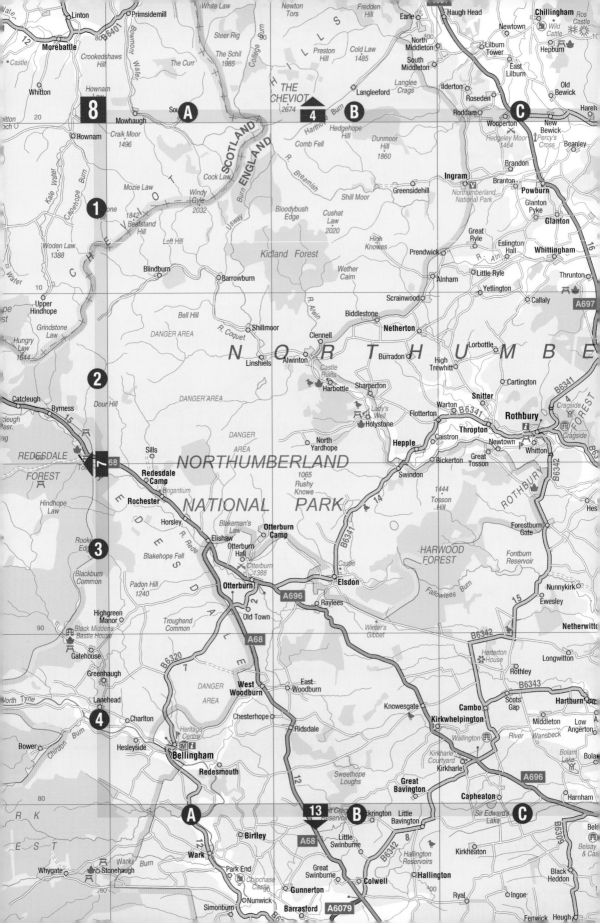

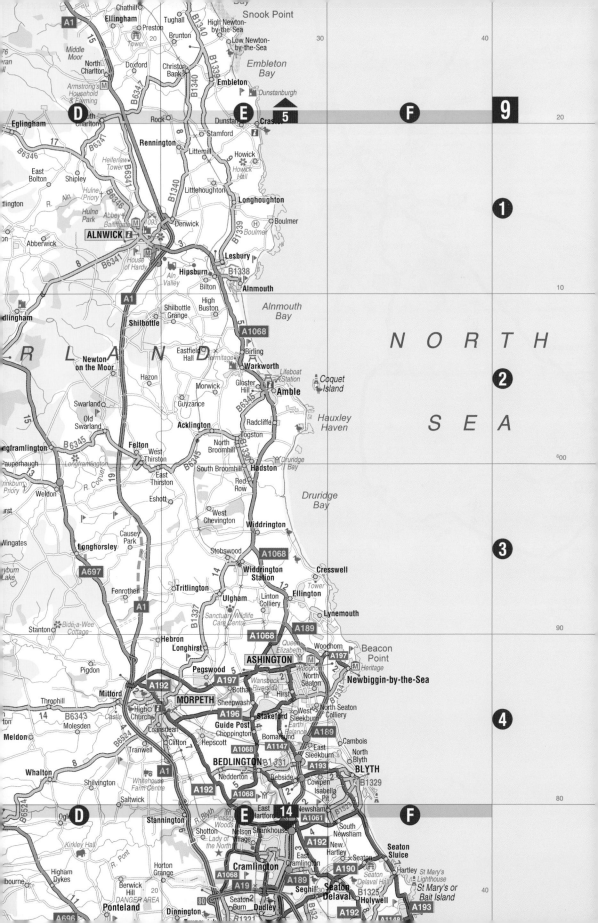

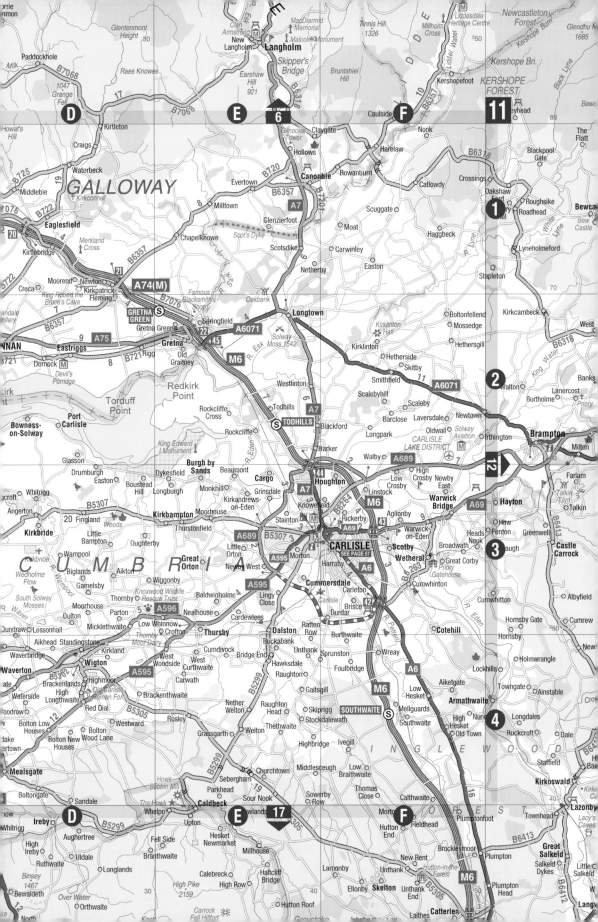

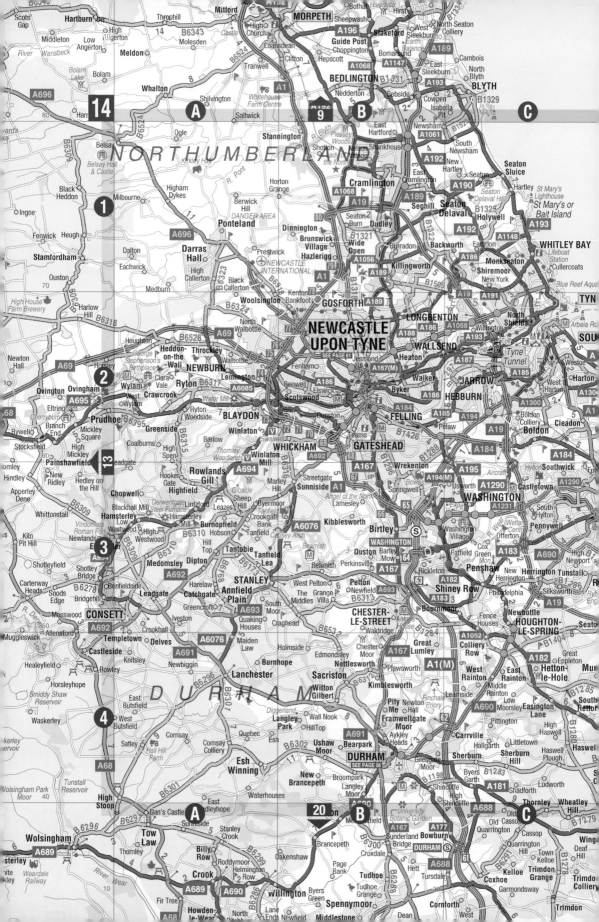

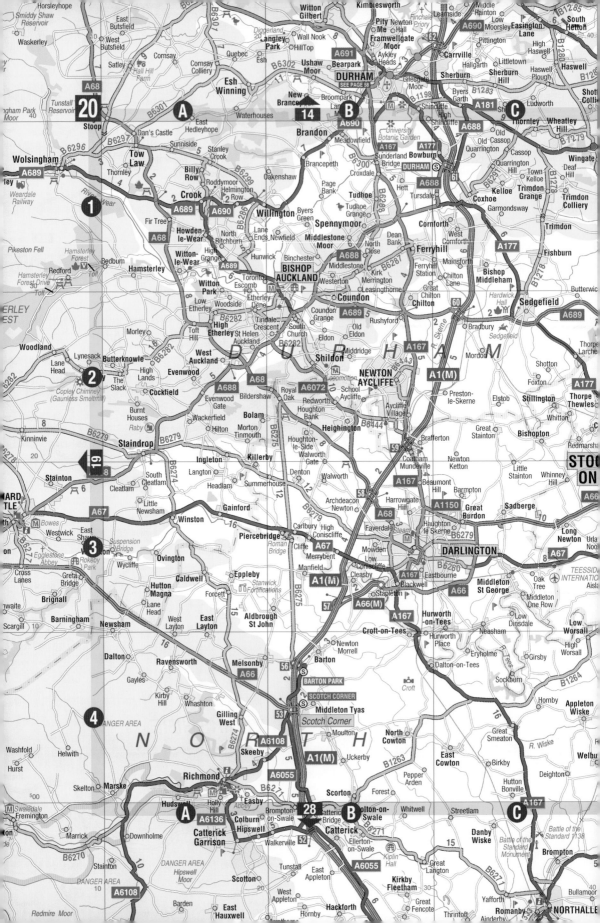

10 20 30

D **E** **F** **23** 40

1 30

S E A

2 20

3 10

4 ⁵00

D **E** **31** **F**

tondale

Peak or
Cheek

Cloughton
Newlands

Cloughton

Burniston

10 20 30

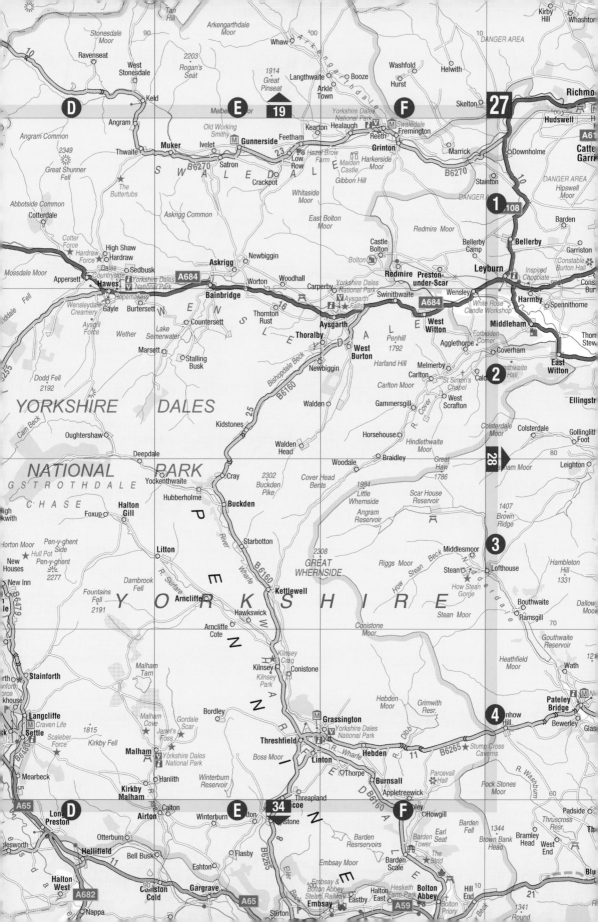

Peak or
Cheek

N O R T H

S E A

1

90

2

80

3

70

4

60

Cloughton
Newlands

Cloughton

Burniston

A171 A165
Scalby
Mills
Sea Life
North Bay Railway

by   Newby
roxenby   Rotunda
arrowcliff   Art Gallery
Falsgrave
SCARBOROUGH

A170

utton Farm   Osgodby   *Cayton Bay*
amer Crossgates **Eastfield**
rton   B1261   A165
B1261   **Cayton**   7   *The Wyke*
A64   Lebberston   Gristhorpe
Newbiggin   A1039
Staxton   **Filey**
Flixton Folkton   Lifeboat Station
A1039   Muston
Staxton   Royal   *Primrose*
B1249   Oak   *Valley*
Hunmanby   Hunmanby
Sands
Fordon
Wold   Reighton
Newton   Speeton
Foxholes
B1249   **Burton**   Buckton
Fleming   B1229   **Bempton**
Grindale   *Danes Dyke*
Octon   **Thwing**   Sewerby   Marton
Hall   **Sewerby**
B1253   Boynton   B1255   Bondville
Rudston   Model Village
Langtoft   Monolith   *Gypsey Race*   Bayle
EAST RIDING   M   **BRIDLINGTON**
A165   **West Hill**
A614   Harbour Heritage
Carnaby   Bessingby   *Lifeboat Station*
Haisthorpe   **Hilderthorpe**
West   **Kilham**   Thornholme   Wilsthorpe
End   John Bull   A1038
Norman   World   Bridlington
Manor House   of Rock   Birds of Prey
Burton
Agnes
OF YORKSHIRE   Harpham   Fraisthorpe
Ruston
Parva
Great   A614   Lowthorpe   Little
Kendale   Kelk   Gransmoor
D   **Natferton**   Great   **Barms**   **38**   **F**
Kelk   **Lissett**
DRIFFIELD   B1242
Wansford   East
End
West
Gembling   End   **Ulrome**
Foston on   A165   *Skipsea*
the Wolds   Dringhoe   **Skipsea**
A164   Skerne   **Beeford**   Upton
Hutton   B1249   Skipsea
Brigham   Brough

FLAMBOROUGH
HEAD

B1255   B1259
Flamborough
Lifeboat
Station

Bridlington

Bay

500

10   20   30

20   30

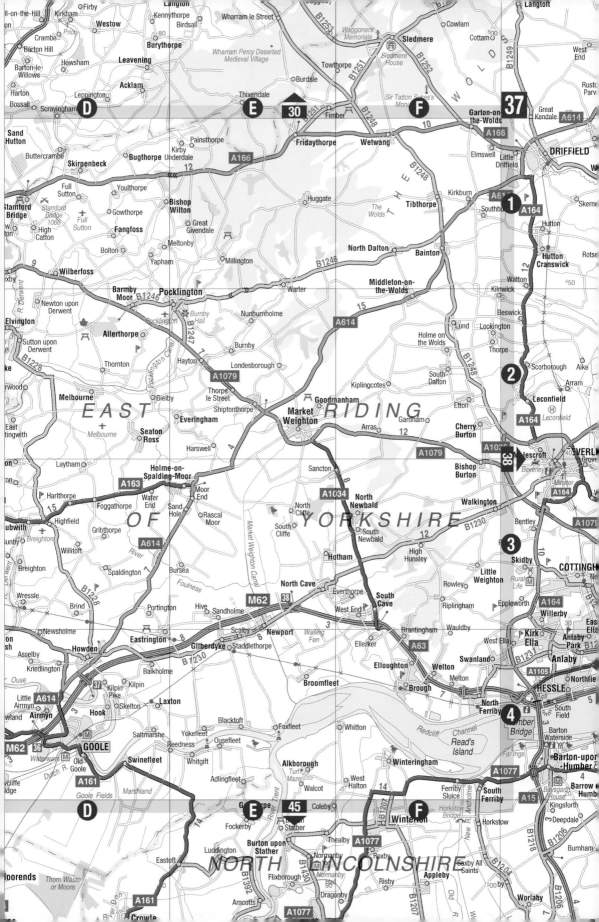

40   ⁵50   60   **39**   60

D   **E**   **F**

①

⁴50

②

40

N   O   R   T   H

S   E   A

③

30

Tunstall

Waxholme

swell   Owthorne

Withernsea

Hollym

Winestead

A1033   **Holmpton**

gton   RAF   Out
         Holmpton Newton
Welwick

B1445   Weeton

④

20

D keffling   **E**   **47** ▼   **F**

Easington

*Sunk Island
Sands*

Kilnsea   Spurn
            Heritage Coast

40   ⁵50   60

*Trinity
Sands*

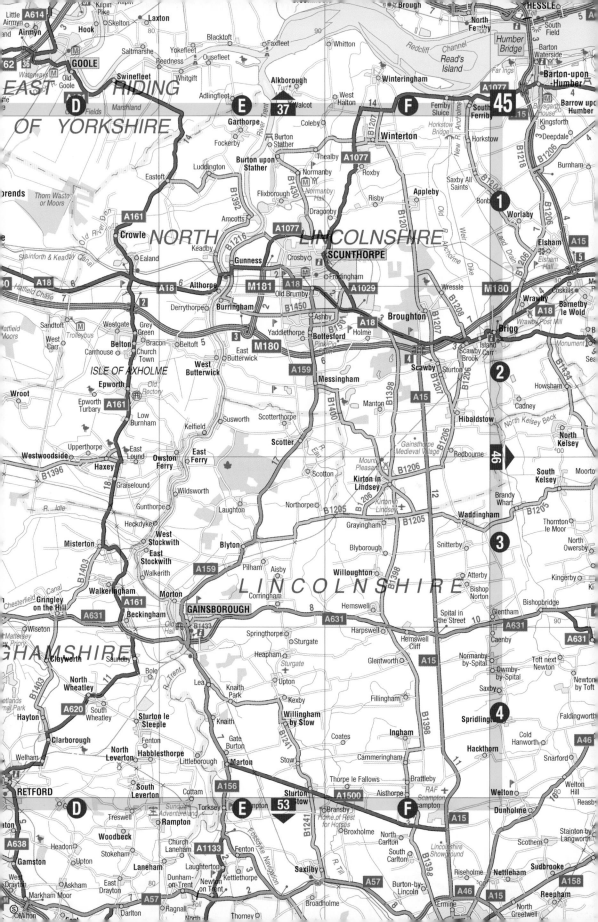

Winestead
Hollym
Holmpton
A1033
RIDING
YORKSHIRE
Welwick
Weeton
B1445
Out
Newton
D
Skeffling
Easington
Sunk Island
Sands
Kilnsea
Spurn
Heritage Coast
Trinity
Sands
Spurn
SPURN
HEAD

180

CLEETHORPES
Discovery Centre
Jungle
A1098
Cleethorpes Coast
Light Railway
Humberston
A1031
Tetney
High Sands
DANGER
AREA
North Cotes
201
Tetney
Lock
Tetney
North
Cotes
Donna
Nook
Fulstow
Marshchapel
18
Eskham
Lincolnshire
Wolds Railway
Grainthorpe
North
Somercotes
DANGER AREA
Grainthorpe
Fen
Conisholme
Church
End
Skidbrooke
North End
Covenham St
Bartholomew
Covenham
St Mary
Austin
Fen
South
Somercotes
A1031
Saltfleet
HIRE
Fotherby
Yarburgh
Skidbrooke
E
Little
Grimsby
Alvingham
North
Cockerington
Saltfleetby
St Clement
A16
Keddington
Corner
Saltfleetby
St Peter
Saltfleetby
All Saints
11
Theddlethorpe
St Helen
Keddington
South
Cockerington
Grimoldby
Three
Bridges
Theddlethorpe
All Saints
Seal Sanctuary
& Wildlife Centre
LOUTH
Stewton
B1200
Manby
Meers
Bridge
Lifeboat
Station
Great
Carlton
Mablethorpe
Ye Olde
Curiosity
Legbourne
Little
Carlton
Gayton
le Marsh
A157
Little
Cawthorpe
South
Reston
Witham
Strubby
A1104
Trusthorpe
Thorpe
Tathwell
12
Tothill
Strubby
Maltby
le Marsh
Sutton on Sea
Haugham
Muckton
Authorpe
Woodthorpe
Beesby
A1111
Sandilands
Maidenwell
Burwell
A16
Belleau
Claythorpe
Clathorpe Watermill
& Wildfowl Gardens
Hannah
A52
Farforth
Ruckland
White
Pit
Aby
Saleby
Markby
Oxcombe
Swaby
South
Thoresby
Bilsby
Huttoft
Anderby
Ketsby
Manor
House
Anderby
Creek
Tetford
South
Ormsby
Calceby
Haugh
Rigsby
Thurlby
Alford
B1449
On Your Marques
Brinkhill
Driby
Well
B1196
Farlesthorpe
13
Mumby
Authorpe
Row
Salmonby
Somersby
A1104
Ulceby
Mawthorpe
Bonthorpe
Cumberworth
Helsey

Hull to:
Rotterdam (Europoort) 10hrs.
Zeebrugge 12hrs. 30mins.

N O R T H

S E A

Mouth of the Humber

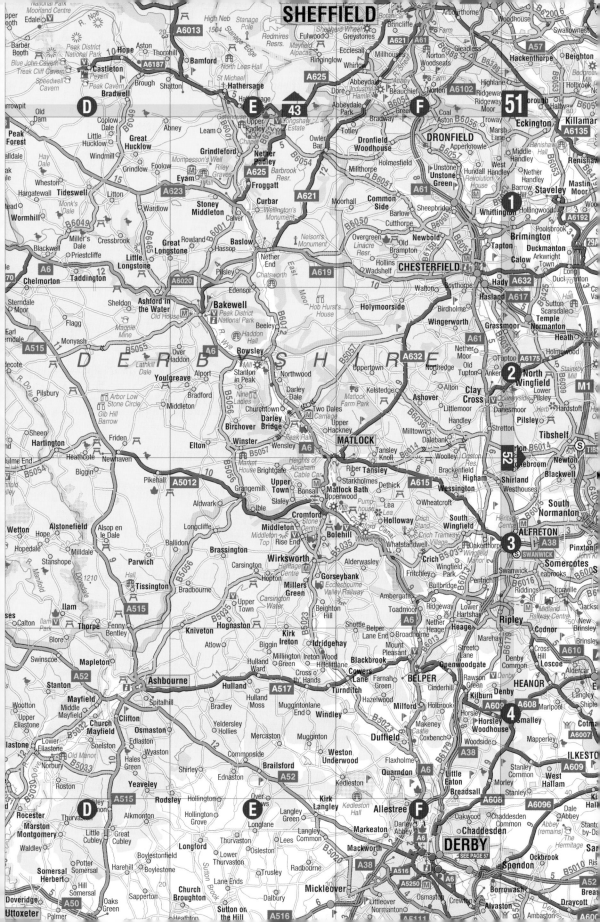

CITY & TOWN CENTRE PLANS

Reference to Town Plans

Motorway ___ **M6**
Motorway Under Construction ___
Motorway Junctions with Numbers ___ **4** **5**
  Unlimited Interchange **4** Limited Interchange **5**
Primary Route ___ **A55**
Dual Carriageways ___
Class A Road ___ A675
Class B Road ___ B5248
Major Roads Under Construction ___
Major Roads Proposed ___
Minor Roads ___
Fuel Station ___
Restricted Access ___
Pedestrianized Road & Main Footway ___
One Way Street ___
Toll ___ Toll
Railway and Station ___
Underground / Metro & D.L.R. Station ___ DLR
Level Crossing and Tunnel ___
Tram Stop and One Way Tram Stop ___
Built-up Area ___

Abbey, Cathedral, Priory etc. ___ ✝
Bus Station ___
Car Park (Selection of) ___ P
Church ___ ✝
City Wall ___
Ferry ___ (vehicular) ⛴ (foot only) 🚶
Golf Course ___
Heliport ___
Hospital ___ H
Lighthouse ___
Market ___
National Trust Property ___ (open) NT ___ (Restricted Opening) NT
  (National Trust of Scotland) NTS NTS
Park & Ride ___ P+R
Place of Interest ___
Police Station ___ ▲
Post Office ___ ★
Shopping Area (Main street and precinct) ___
Shopmobility ___
Toilet ___ ▽
Tourist Information Centre ___ i
Viewpoint ___
Visitor Information Centre ___ V

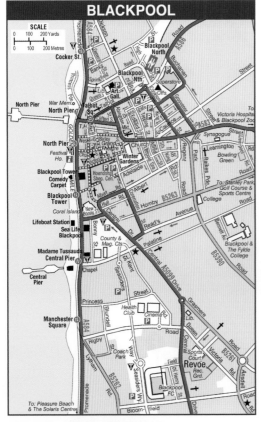

BLACKPOOL

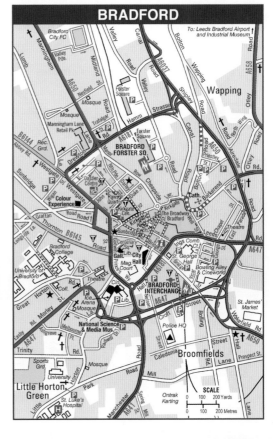

BRADFORD

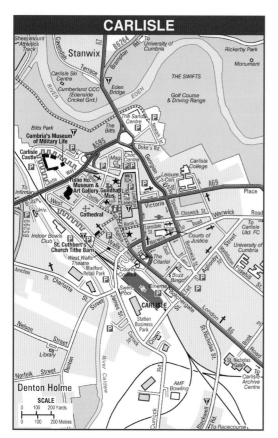

CARLISLE

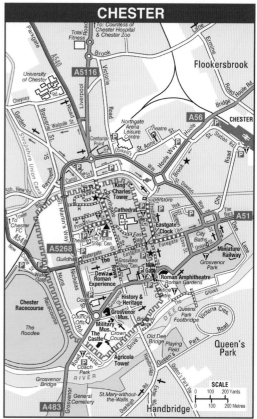

CHESTER

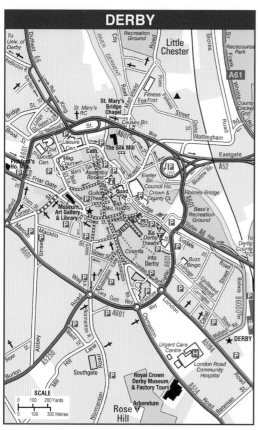

DERBY

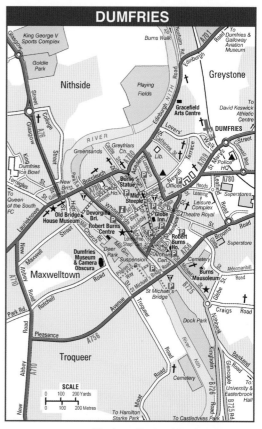

DUMFRIES

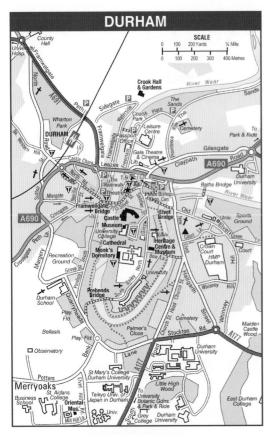

DURHAM

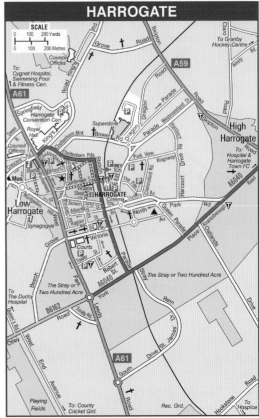

HARROGATE

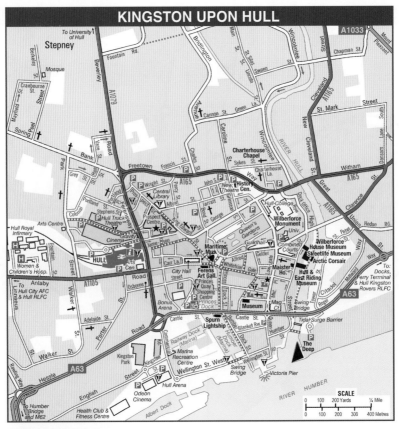

KINGSTON UPON HULL

58 Northern England Regional Atlas

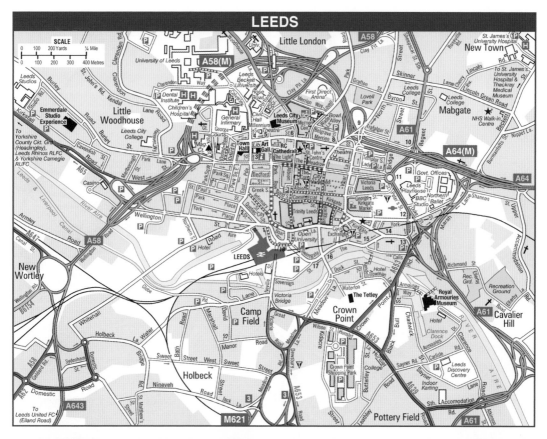

LEEDS

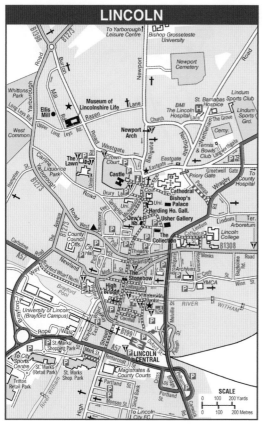

LINCOLN

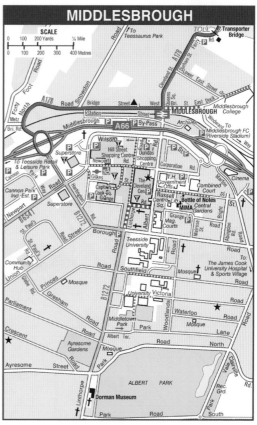

MIDDLESBROUGH

LIVERPOOL

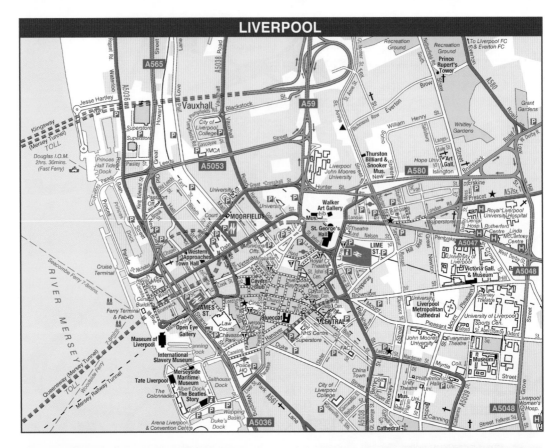

MANCHESTER

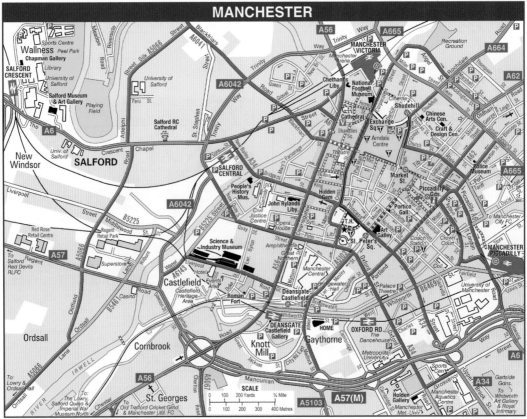

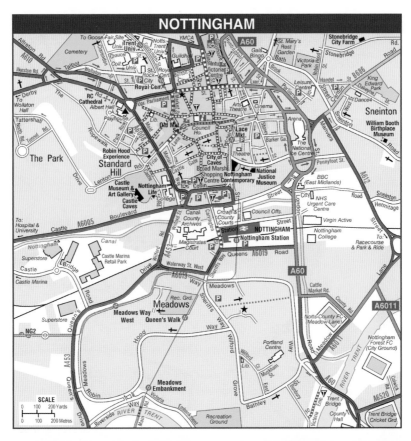

NOTTINGHAM

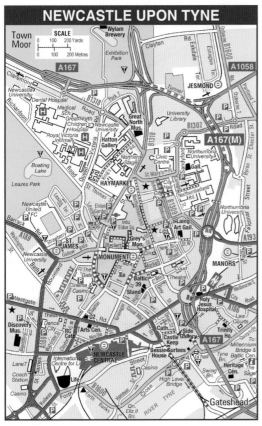

NEWCASTLE UPON TYNE

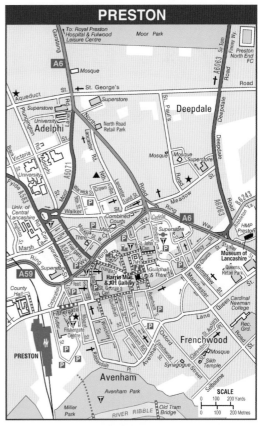

PRESTON

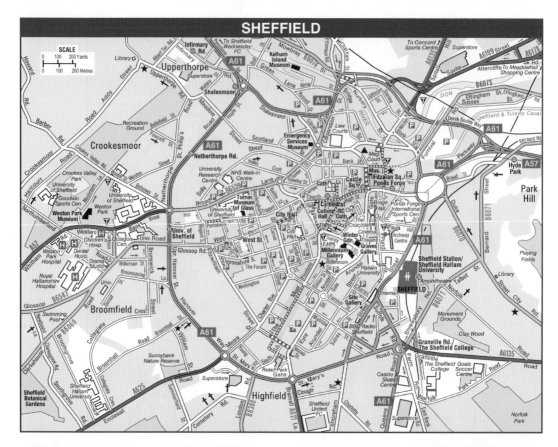

SHEFFIELD

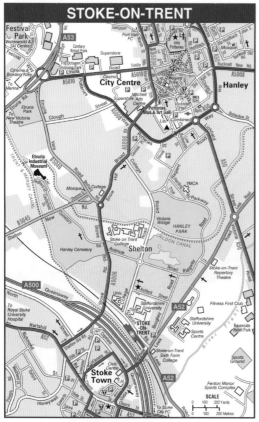

STOKE-ON-TRENT

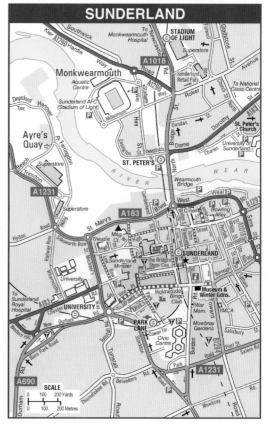

SUNDERLAND

62 Northern England Regional Atlas

YORK

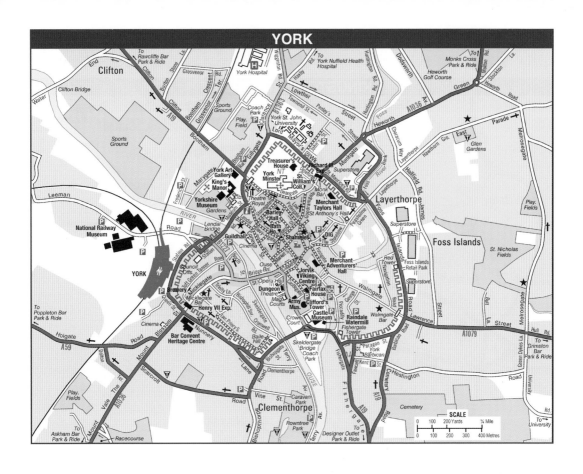

MANCHESTER AIRPORT

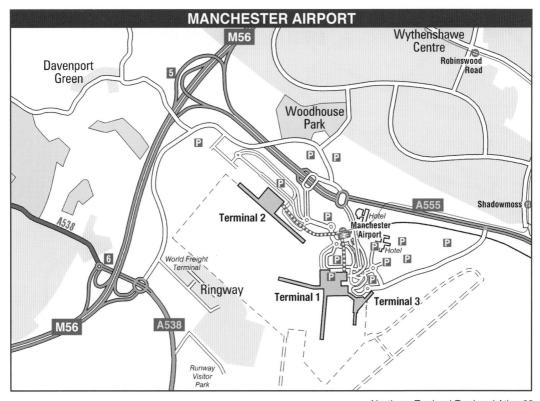

KINGSTON UPON HULL

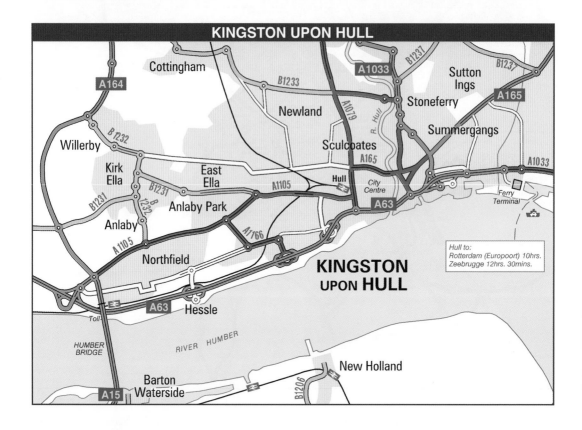

Cottingham

A164

B1233

A1033

B1237

Sutton Ings

B1237

A165

Stoneferry

Willerby

B1232

Newland

A1079

Summergangs

A1033

Kirk Ella

B1231

B1232

East Ella

A1105

Sculcoates

R. Hull

A165

Anlaby Park

Hull

City Centre

Ferry Terminal

Anlaby

A1105

A1166

A63

Northfield

KINGSTON
UPON HULL

Hull to:
Rotterdam (Europoort) 10hrs.
Zeebrugge 12hrs. 30mins.

A63

Hessle

Toll

HUMBER BRIDGE

RIVER HUMBER

New Holland

Barton Waterside

A15

B1206

NEWCASTLE UPON TYNE

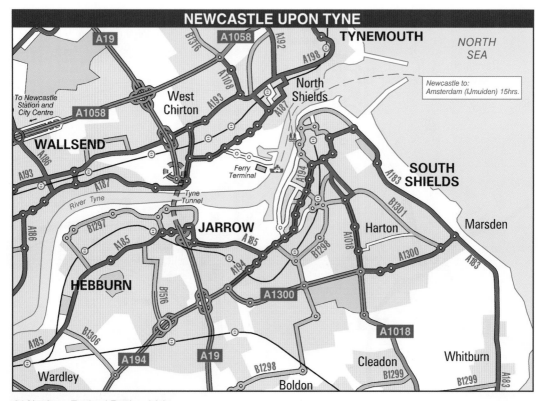

A19

B1316

A1058

A192

A198

TYNEMOUTH

NORTH SEA

A1108

North Shields

Newcastle to:
Amsterdam (IJmuiden) 15hrs.

To Newcastle Station and City Centre

A1058

West Chirton

A193

A187

WALLSEND

A186

A193

A187

Ferry Terminal

Tyne Tunnel

River Tyne

SOUTH SHIELDS

A183

A194

A186

B1297

A185

JARROW

A185

B1301

Harton

Marsden

B1298

A1018

A1300

A183

HEBBURN

B1516

A194

A1300

A1018

A185

B1306

A194

A19

B1298

Cleadon

Whitburn

Wardley

Boldon

B1299

B1299

A183

INDEX TO CITIES, TOWNS, VILLAGES, HAMLETS & LOCATIONS

1. A strict alphabetical order is used e.g. Ashover follows Ash Magna but precedes Ash Parva.
2. The map reference given refers to the actual map square in which the town spot or built-up area is located and not to the place name.
3. Major towns, selected airports and ports are shown in bold, i.e. **Blackpool** Bkpl ...... 3B **32** & **56**. Where they appear on a town plan a second page reference is given.
4. Where two places of the same name occur in the same County or Unitary Authority, the nearest large town is also given; e.g. Aisby. Linc ...... 3E **45** (nr. Gainsborough) indicates that Aisby is located in square 3E on page **45** and is situated near Gainsborough in the County of Lincolnshire.
5. Only one reference is given although due to page overlaps the place may appear on more than one page.

COUNTIES AND UNITARY AUTHORITIES with the abbreviations used in this index.

Blackburn with Darwen : *Bkbn*
Blackpool : *Bkpl*
Cheshire East : *Ches E*
Cheshire West & Chester : *Ches W*
Cumbria : *Cumb*
Darlington : *Darl*
Denbighshire : *Den*
Derby : *Derb*

Derbyshire : *Derbs*
Dumfries & Galloway : *Dum*
Durham : *Dur*
East Riding of Yorkshire : *E Yor*
Flintshire : *Flin*
Greater Manchester : *G Man*
Halton : *Hal*
Hartlepool : *Hart*

Kingston upon Hull : *Hull*
Lancashire : *Lanc*
Leicestershire : *Leics*
Lincolnshire : *Linc*
Merseyside : *Mers*
Middlesbrough : *Midd*
North East Lincolnshire : *NE Lin*
North Lincolnshire : *N Lin*

Northumberland : *Nmbd*
North Yorkshire : *N Yor*
Nottingham : *Nott*
Nottinghamshire : *Notts*
Redcar & Cleveland : *Red C*
Scottish Borders : *Bord*
Shropshire : *Shrp*
South Yorkshire : *S Yor*

Staffordshire : *Staf*
Stockton-on-Tees : *Stoc T*
Stoke-on-Trent : *Stoke*
Tyne & Wear : *Tyne*
Warrington : *Warr*
West Yorkshire : *W Yor*
Wrexham : *Wrex*
York : *York*

INDEX

Barmpton – Breaden Heath

Barmpton *Darl* 3C 20
Barmston *E Yor* 1B 38
Barnard Castle *Dur* 3F 19
Barnburgh *S Yor* 2A 44
Barnby Dun *S Yor* 2C 44
Barnby in the Willows *Notts* 3E 53
Barnby Moor *Notts* 4C 44
Barnetby le Wold *N Lin* 2A 46
Barningham *Dur* 3F 19
Barnoldby le Beck *NE Lin* 2C 46
Barnoldswick *Lanc* 2A 34
Barnsley *S Yor* 2F 43
Barnston *Mers* 4A 40
Barnstone *Notts* 4D 53
Barnton *Ches W* 1E 49
Barrasford *Nmbd* 1E 13
Barrow *Lanc* 3F 33
Barrow Bridge *G Man* 1E 41
Barrowburn *Nmbd* 1A 8
Barrowby *Linc* 4E 53
Barrowcliff *N Yor* 2D 31
Barrowford *Lanc* 3A 34
Barrow Haven *N Lin* 4A 38
Barrow Hill *Derbs* 1A 52
Barrow-in-Furness *Cumb* 4D 25
Barrow Nook *Lanc* 2C 40
Barrow's Green *Hal* 4D 41
Barrows Green *Cumb* 2A 26
Barrow upon Humber *N Lin* 4A 38
Barthomley *Ches E* 3F 49
Barton *Ches W* 3C 48
Barton *Cumb* 2F 17
Barton *Lanc* 2B 40
(nr Ormskirk)
Barton *Lanc* 3D 33
(nr Preston)
Barton *N Yor* 4B 20
Barton Hill *N Yor* 4A 30
Barton-le-Street *N Yor* 3A 30
Barton-le-Willows *N Yor* 4A 30
Barton-upon-Humber *N Lin* 4A 38
Barton Waterside *N Lin* 4A 38
Barugh Green *S Yor* 2F 43
Barwick in Elmet *W Yor* 3F 35
Basford Green *Staf* 3B 50
Bashall Eaves *Lanc* 2E 33
Bashall Town *Lanc* 2F 33
Baslow *Derbs* 1E 51
Bassenthwaite *Cumb* 1D 17
Bassingfield *Notts* 4C 52
Bassingham *Linc* 2F 53
Bate Heath *Ches E* 1E 49
Bathley *Notts* 3D 53
Batley *W Yor* 4E 35
Battersby *N Yor* 4E 21
Baumber *Linc* 1C 54
Bawtry *S Yor* 3C 44
Baxenden *Lanc* 4F 33
Baybridge *Nmbd* 3E 13
Baycliff *Cumb* 3D 25
Bayles *Cumb* 4C 12
Baythorpe *Linc* 4C 54
Beadlam *N Yor* 2F 29
Beadnell *Nmbd* 4E 5
Beal *N Yor* 4B 36
Beal *Nmbd* 2C 4
Beamhurst *Staf* 4C 50
Beamish *Dur* 3B 14
Beamsley *N Yor* 1C 34
Beanley *Nmbd* 1C 8
Beardwood *Bkbn* 4E 33
Bearpark *Dur* 4B 14
Bearsbridge *Nmbd* 3C 12
Bearstone *Shrp* 4F 49
Beauchief *S Yor* 4F 43
Beaumont *Cumb* 3E 11
Beaumont Hill *Darl* 3B 20
Beauvale *Notts* 4A 52
Bebington *Mers* 4B 40
Bebside *Nmbd* 4E 9
Becconsall *Lanc* 4C 32
Beckermet *Cumb* 4B 16
Beck Foot *Cumb* 1B 26
Beckfoot *Cumb* 2C 24
(nr Broughton in Furness)
Beckfoot *Cumb* 4C 16
(nr Seascale)
Beckfoot *Cumb* 4B 10
(nr Silloth)
Beck Hole *N Yor* 4B 22
Beckingham *Linc* 3E 53
Beckingham *Notts* 3D 45
Beck Side *Cumb* 2E 25
(nr Cartmel)
Beck Side *Cumb* 2D 25
(nr Ulverston)
Beckside *Cumb* 2B 26
Beckwithshaw *N Yor* 1E 35
Bedale *N Yor* 2B 28
Bedburn *Dur* 1A 20
Bedford *G Man* 3E 41
Bedlam *N Yor* 4B 28
Bedlington *Nmbd* 4E 9
Bedrule *Bord* 1E 7
Beech *Staf* 4A 50
Beechcliffe *W Yor* 2C 34
Beeford *E Yor* 1B 38
Beeley *Derbs* 2E 51
Beelsby *NE Lin* 2C 46
Beesby *Linc* 4E 47
Beeston *Ches W* 3D 49
Beeston *Notts* 4B 52
Beeston *W Yor* 3E 35
Beeswing *Dum* 2A 10
Beetham *Cumb* 3F 25
Beighton *S Yor* 4A 44
Beighton Hill *Derbs* 3E 51
Belchford *Linc* 1C 54
Belford *Nmbd* 3D 5
Bell Busk *N Yor* 1B 34
Belleau *Linc* 1E 55
Bellerby *N Yor* 1A 28
Bellerby Camp *N Yor* 1F 27
Belle Vue *Cumb* 1C 16
Bellingham *Nmbd* 4A 8
Bellshill *Nmbd* 3D 5
Belmont *Bkbn* 1E 41
Belper *Derbs* 4F 51
Belper Lane End *Derbs* 4F 51
Belph *Derbs* 1B 52
Belsay *Nmbd* 1A 14
Belthorn *Lanc* 4F 33
Beltoft *N Lin* 2E 45
Belton *Linc* 4F 53
Belton *N Lin* 2D 45
Belvoir *Leics* 4E 53
Bempton *E Yor* 3E 31
Benchill *G Man* 4A 42
Benfieldside *Dur* 3F 13
Beningbrough *N Yor* 1B 36
Benington *Linc* 4D 55
Benington Sea End *Linc* 4E 55
Bennethead *Cumb* 2F 17
Benniworth *Linc* 4C 46
Bentley *E Yor* 3A 38
Bentley *S Yor* 2B 44
Bentpath *Dum* 3B 6
Benwell *Tyne* 2B 14
Berrier *Cumb* 2E 17
Berrington *Nmbd* 2C 4
Berrington Law *Nmbd* 2B 4
Berryscaur *Dum* 3A 6
Bersham *Wrex* 4B 48
Berwick Hill *Nmbd* 1A 14
Berwick-upon-Tweed *Nmbd* 1B 4
Berwyn *Den* 4A 48
Bescar *Lanc* 1B 40
Bessacarr *S Yor* 2C 44
Bessingby *E Yor* 4E 31
Besthorpe *Notts* 2E 53
Bestwood Village *Notts* 4B 52
Beswick *E Yor* 2A 38
Betley *Staf* 4F 49
Bettisfield *Wrex* 4C 48
Betton *Shrp* 4E 49
Bevercotes *Notts* 1D 53
Beverley *E Yor* 3A 38
Bewaldeth *Cumb* 1D 17
Bewcastle *Cumb* 1A 12
Bewerley *N Yor* 4A 28
Bewholme *E Yor* 1B 38
Bibbington *Derbs* 1C 50
Bicker *Linc* 4C 54
Bicker Bar *Linc* 4C 54
Bicker Gauntlet *Linc* 4C 54
Bickershaw *G Man* 2E 41
Bickerstaffe *Lanc* 2C 40
Bickerton *Ches E* 3D 49
Bickerton *N Yor* 1A 36
Bickerton *Nmbd* 2B 8
Bickley *N Yor* 1C 30
Bickley Moss *Ches W* 4D 49
Biddlestone *Nmbd* 2B 8
Biddulph *Staf* 3A 50
Biddulph Moor *Staf* 3B 50
Bidston *Mers* 4A 40
Bielby *E Yor* 2D 37
Bierley *W Yor* 3D 35
Bigby *Linc* 2A 46
Biggar *Cumb* 4C 24
Biggin *Derbs* 3D 51
(nr Hartington)
Biggin *Derbs* 4E 51
(nr Hulland)
Biggin *N Yor* 3B 36
Biglands *Cumb* 3D 11
Bignall End *Staf* 3A 50
Bigrigg *Cumb* 3B 16
Bilborough *Nott* 4B 52
Bilbrough *N Yor* 2B 36
Bilby *Notts* 4C 44
Bildershaw *Dur* 2B 20
Billingborough *Linc* 4B 54
Billinge *Mers* 2D 41
Billingham *Stoc T* 2D 21
Billinghay *Linc* 3B 54
Billingley *S Yor* 2A 44
Billington *Lanc* 3F 33
Billy Row *Dur* 1A 20
Bilsborrow *Lanc* 2D 33
Bilsby *Linc* 1E 55
Bilsthorpe *Notts* 2C 52
Bilton *E Yor* 3B 38
Bilton *N Yor* 1F 35
Bilton *Nmbd* 1E 9
Bilton in Ainsty *N Yor* 2A 36
Binbrook *Linc* 3C 46
Binchester *Dur* 1B 20
Bingfield *Nmbd* 1E 13
Bingham *Notts* 4D 53
Bingley *W Yor* 3D 35
Binsoe *N Yor* 3B 28
Birch *G Man* 2A 42
Birchall *Staf* 3B 50
Birch Heath *Ches W* 2D 49
Birch Hill *Ches W* 1D 49
Birchover *Derbs* 2E 51
Birch Vale *Derbs* 4C 42
Birchwood *Linc* 2F 53
Birchwood *Warr* 3E 41
Bircotes *Notts* 3C 44
Birdholme *Derbs* 2F 51
Birdsall *N Yor* 4B 30
Birds Edge *W Yor* 2E 43
Birdwell *S Yor* 2F 43
Birgham *Bord* 3A 4
Birkby *Cumb* 1B 16
Birkby *N Yor* 4C 20
Birkdale *Mers* 1B 40
Birkenhead *Mers* 4B 40
Birkenshaw *W Yor* 4E 35
Birkin *N Yor* 4B 36
Birling *Nmbd* 2E 9
Birstall *W Yor* 4E 35
Birstall Smithies *W Yor* 4E 35
Birstwith *N Yor* 1E 35
Birthorpe *Linc* 4B 54
Birtle *G Man* 1A 42
Birtley *Nmbd* 1D 13
Birtley *Tyne* 3B 14
Bishop Auckland *Dur* 2B 20
Bishopbridge *Linc* 3A 46
Bishop Burton *E Yor* 3F 37
Bishop Middleham *Dur* 1C 20
Bishop Monkton *N Yor* 4C 28
Bishop Norton *Linc* 3F 45
Bishop Thornton *N Yor* 4B 28
Bishopthorpe *York* 2B 36
Bishopton *Darl* 2C 20
Bishopton *N Yor* 3B 28
Bishop Wilton *E Yor* 1D 37
Bispham *Bkpl* 2B 32
Bispham Green *Lanc* 1C 40
Blackbrook *Derbs* 4F 51
Blackbrook *Mers* 3D 41
Blackbrook *Staf* 4F 49
Blackburn *Bkbn* 4E 33
Black Callerton *Tyne* 2A 14
Blackden Heath *Ches E* 1F 49
Blackdyke *Cumb* 3C 10
Blacker Hill *S Yor* 2F 43
Blackford *Cumb* 2E 11
Blackhall Colliery *Dur* 1D 21
Blackhall Mill *Tyne* 3A 14
Blackhall Rocks *Dur* 1D 21
Black Heddon *Nmbd* 1F 13
Blackjack *Linc* 4C 54
Black Lane *G Man* 2F 41
Blackleach *Lanc* 3C 32
Blackley *G Man* 2A 42
Blackley *W Yor* 1D 43
Blackmoor *G Man* 2E 41
Blacko *Lanc* 2A 34
Blackpool *Bkpl* 3B 32 & 56
Blackpool Gate *Cumb* 1A 12
Blackrod *G Man* 1E 41
Blackshaw *Dum* 2B 10
Blackshaw Head *W Yor* 4B 34
Blackshaw Moor *Staf* 3C 50
Blacksnape *Bkbn* 4F 33
Blacktoft *E Yor* 4E 37
Blackwell *Darl* 3B 20
Blackwell *Derbs* 3A 52
(nr Alfreton)
Blackwell *Derbs* 1D 51
(nr Buxton)
Blackwood Hill *Staf* 3B 50
Blacon *Ches W* 2B 48
Blagill *Cumb* 4C 12
Blaguegate *Lanc* 2C 40
Blakenhall *Ches E* 4F 49
Blanchland *Nmbd* 3E 13
Bland Hill *N Yor* 1E 35
Blankney *Linc* 2A 54
Blawith *Cumb* 2D 25
Blaxton *S Yor* 2C 44
Blaydon *Tyne* 2A 14
Bleasby *Linc* 4B 46
Bleasby *Notts* 4D 53
Bleasby Moor *Linc* 4B 46
Blencarn *Cumb* 1B 18
Blencogo *Cumb* 4C 10
Blennerhasset *Cumb* 4C 10
Bletchley *Shrp* 4E 49
Blidworth *Notts* 3B 52
Blindburn *Nmbd* 1A 8
Blindcrake *Cumb* 1C 16
Blitterlees *Cumb* 3C 10
Bloomfield *Bord* 1D 7
Blore *Staf* 4D 51
Bloxholm *Linc* 3A 54
Blubberhouses *N Yor* 1D 35
Blurton *Stoke* 4A 50
Blyborough *Linc* 3F 45
Blyth *Nmbd* 4F 9
Blyth *Notts* 4C 44
Blythe Bridge *Staf* 4B 50
Blythe Marsh *Staf* 4B 50
Blyton *Linc* 3E 45
Boar's Head *G Man* 2D 41
Bolam *Dur* 2A 20
Bolam *Nmbd* 4C 8
Bold Heath *Mers* 4D 41
Boldon *Tyne* 2C 14
Boldon Colliery *Tyne* 2C 14
Boldron *Dur* 3F 19
Bole *Notts* 4D 45
Bolehill *Derbs* 3E 51
Bollington *Ches E* 1B 50
Bolsover *Derbs* 1A 52
Bolsterstone *S Yor* 3E 43
Boltby *N Yor* 2D 29
Bolton *Cumb* 2B 18
Bolton *E Yor* 1D 37
Bolton *G Man* 2F 41
Bolton *Nmbd* 1D 9
Bolton Abbey *N Yor* 1C 34
Bolton-by-Bowland *Lanc* 2F 33
Boltonfellend *Cumb* 2F 11
Boltongate *Cumb* 4D 11
Bolton Green *Lanc* 1D 41
Bolton-le-Sands *Lanc* 4F 25
Bolton Low Houses *Cumb* 4D 11
Bolton New Houses *Cumb* 4D 11
Bolton-on-Swale *N Yor* 1B 28
Bolton Percy *N Yor* 2B 36
Bolton Town End *Lanc* 4F 25
Bolton upon Dearne *S Yor* 2A 44
Bolton Wood Lane *Cumb* 4D 11
Bomarsund *Nmbd* 4E 9
Bonby *N Lin* 1A 46
Bonchester Bridge *Bord* 1D 7
Bonds *Lanc* 2C 32
Bonjedward *Bord* 1E 7
Bonsall *Derbs* 3E 51
Bonthorpe *Linc* 1E 55
Boosbeck *Red C* 3F 21
Boot *Cumb* 4C 16
Booth *W Yor* 4C 34
Boothby Graffoe *Linc* 3F 53
Booth Green *Ches E* 4B 42
Boothstown *G Man* 2F 41
Bootle *Cumb* 2C 24
Bootle *Mers* 3B 40
Booze *N Yor* 4F 19
Bordley *N Yor* 4E 27
Boreland *Dum* 3A 6
Boroughbridge *N Yor* 4C 28
Borrowash *Derbs* 4A 52
Borrowby *N Yor* 2D 29
(nr Northallerton)
Borrowby *N Yor* 3A 22
(nr Whitby)
Borwick *Lanc* 3A 26
Bosley *Ches E* 2B 50
Bossall *N Yor* 4A 30
Bostock Green *Ches W* 2E 49
Boston *Linc* 4D 55
Boston Spa *W Yor* 2A 36
Bothal *Nmbd* 4E 9
Bothamsall *Notts* 1C 52
Bothel *Cumb* 1C 16
Bottesford *Leics* 4E 53
Bottesford *N Lin* 2E 45
Bottom o' th' Moor *G Man* 1E 41
Botton *N Yor* 4F 21
Botton Head *Lanc* 4B 26
Boughton *Notts* 2C 52
Boulby *Red C* 3A 22
Boulmer *Nmbd* 1E 9
Boultham *Linc* 2F 53
Boundary *Staf* 4B 50
Bournmoor *Dur* 3C 14
Boustead Hill *Cumb* 3D 11
Bouth *Cumb* 2E 25
Bouthwaite *N Yor* 3A 28
Bowbank *Dur* 2E 19
Bowburn *Dur* 1C 20
Bowderdale *Cumb* 4B 18
Bowdon *G Man* 4F 41
Bower *Nmbd* 4F 7
Bowers *Staf* 4A 50
Bowes *Dur* 3E 19
Bowgreave *Lanc* 2C 32
Bowland Bridge *Cumb* 2F 25
Bowlees *Dur* 2E 19
Bowling *W Yor* 3D 35
Bowling Bank *Wrex* 4B 48
Bowmanstead *Cumb* 1E 25
Bowness-on-Solway *Cumb* 2D 11
Bowness-on-Windermere *Cumb* 1F 25
Bowscale *Cumb* 1E 17
Bowsden *Nmbd* 2B 4
Bowston *Cumb* 1F 25
Boylestone *Derbs* 4D 51
Boylestonfield *Derbs* 4D 51
Boynton *E Yor* 4E 31
Boythorpe *Derbs* 2F 51
Bracebridge *Linc* 2F 53
Bracebridge Heath *Linc* 2F 53
Braceby *Linc* 4A 54
Bracewell *Lanc* 2A 34
Brackenber *Cumb* 3C 18
Brackenfield *Derbs* 3F 51
Brackenlands *Cumb* 4D 11
Brackenthwaite *Cumb* 4D 11
Brackenthwaite *N Yor* 1E 35
Bracon *N Lin* 2D 45
Bradbourne *Derbs* 3E 51
Bradbury *Dur* 2C 20
Bradfield Green *Ches E* 3E 49
Bradford *Derbs* 2E 51
Bradford *Nmbd* 3D 5
Bradford *W Yor* 3D 35 & 56
Bradley *Ches W* 1D 49
Bradley *Derbs* 4E 51
Bradley *NE Lin* 2C 46
Bradley *W Yor* 4D 35
Bradley *Wrex* 3B 48
Bradley Green *Ches W* 4D 49
Bradley in the Moors *Staf* 4C 50
Bradley Mount *Ches E* 1B 50
Bradnop *Staf* 3C 50
Bradshaw *G Man* 1F 41
Bradwall Green *Ches E* 2F 49
Bradway *S Yor* 4F 43
Bradwell *Derbs* 4D 43
Brafferton *Darl* 2B 20
Brafferton *N Yor* 3D 29
Braides *Lanc* 1C 32
Braidley *N Yor* 2F 27
Brailsford *Derbs* 4E 51
Braithwaite *Cumb* 2D 17
Braithwaite *S Yor* 1C 44
Braithwaite *W Yor* 2C 34
Braithwell *S Yor* 3B 44
Bramcote *Notts* 4B 52
Bramhall *G Man* 4A 42
Bramham *W Yor* 2A 36
Bramhope *W Yor* 2E 35
Bramley *S Yor* 3A 44
Bramley *W Yor* 3E 35
Bramley Head *N Yor* 1D 35
Bramley Vale *Derbs* 2A 52
Brampton *Cumb* 2B 18
(nr Appleby-in-Westmorland)
Brampton *Cumb* 2A 12
(nr Carlisle)
Brampton *Linc* 1E 53
Brampton *S Yor* 2A 44
Brampton en le Morthen *S Yor* 4A 44
Brancepeth *Dur* 1B 20
Branch End *Nmbd* 2F 13
Brand End *Linc* 4D 55
Brandesburton *E Yor* 2B 38
Brandon *Dur* 1B 20
Brandon *Linc* 4F 53
Brandon *Nmbd* 1C 8
Brandsby *N Yor* 3E 29
Brandy Wharf *Linc* 3A 46
Bransby *Linc* 1E 53
Bransholme *Hull* 3B 38
Branston *Linc* 2A 54
Branston Booths *Linc* 2A 54
Bransty *Cumb* 3A 16
Brant Broughton *Linc* 3F 53
Branthwaite *Cumb* 1D 17
(nr Caldbeck)
Branthwaite *Cumb* 2B 16
(nr Workington)
Brantingham *E Yor* 4F 37
Branton *Nmbd* 1C 8
Branton *S Yor* 2C 44
Branton Green *N Yor* 4D 29
Branxholme *Bord* 1C 6
Branxton *Nmbd* 3A 4
Brassington *Derbs* 3E 51
Bratoft *Linc* 2E 55
Brattleby *Linc* 4F 45
Brawby *N Yor* 3A 30
Braystones *Cumb* 4B 16
Brayton *N Yor* 3C 36
Breaden Heath *Shrp* 4C 48

Breadsall – Chirnside

Breadsall *Derbs* 4F **51**
Brearton *N Yor* 4C **28**
Breaston *Derbs* 4A **52**
Bredbury *G Man* 3B **42**
Breightmet *G Man* 2F **41**
Breighton *E Yor* 3D **37**
Brereton Green *Ches E* 2F **49**
Brereton Heath *Ches E* 2A **50**
Bretherdale Head *Cumb* 4A **18**
Bretherton *Lanc* 4C **32**
Bretton *Flin* 2B **48**
Bridekirk *Cumb* 1C **16**
Bridge End *Cumb* 1D **25**
(nr Broughton in Furness)
Bridge End *Cumb* 4E **11**
(nr Dalston)
Bridge End *Linc* 4B **54**
Bridgefoot *Cumb* 2B **16**
Bridge Hewick *N Yor* 3C **28**
Bridgehill *Dur* 3F **13**
Bridgemere *Ches E* 4F **49**
Bridgemont *Derbs* 4C **42**
Bridgend *Cumb* 3E **17**
Bridge Trafford *Ches W* 1C **48**
Bridlington *E Yor* 4E **31**
Brierfield *Lanc* 3A **34**
Brierley *S Yor* 1A **44**
Brierton *Hart* 1D **21**
Briestfield *W Yor* 1E **43**
Brigg *N Lin* 2A **46**
Briggswath *N Yor* 4B **22**
Brigham *Cumb* 1B **16**
Brigham *E Yor* 1A **38**
Brighouse *W Yor* 4D **35**
Brightgate *Derbs* 3E **51**
Brightholmlee *S Yor* 3E **43**
Brignall *Dur* 3F **19**
Brigsley *NE Lin* 2C **46**
Brigsteer *Cumb* 2F **25**
Brimington *Derbs* 1A **52**
Brimstage *Mers* 4B **40**
Brincliffe *S Yor* 4F **43**
Brind *E Yor* 3D **37**
Brindle *Lanc* 4D **33**
Brindley *Ches E* 3D **49**
Brindley Ford *Stoke* 3A **50**
Brinkhill *Linc* 1D **55**
Brinscall *Lanc* 4E **33**
Brinsley *Notts* 4A **52**
Brinsworth *S Yor* 4A **44**
Brisco *Cumb* 3F **11**
Britannia *Lanc* 4A **34**
Broadbottom *G Man* 3B **42**
Broadgate *Cumb* 2C **24**
Broadheath *G Man* 4F **41**
Broadholme *Derbs* 4F **51**
Broadholme *Linc* 1E **53**
Broadley *Lanc* 1A **42**
Broad Oak *Cumb* 1C **24**
Broadwath *Cumb* 3F **11**
Broadwell House *Nmbd* 3E **13**
Brockhill *Bord* 1B **6**
Brockholes *W Yor* 1D **43**
Brocklesby *Linc* 1B **46**
Brockleymoor *Cumb* 1F **17**
Brodsworth *S Yor* 2B **44**
Broken Cross *Ches E* 1A **50**
Bromborough *Mers* 4B **40**
Bromfield *Cumb* 4C **10**
Bromley Cross *G Man* 1F **41**
Brompton *N Yor* 1C **28**
(nr Northallerton)
Brompton *N Yor* 2C **30**
(nr Scarborough)
Brompton-on-Swale *N Yor* 1B **28**
Bronington *Wrex* 4C **48**
Bronygarth *Shrp* 4A **48**
Brookenby *Linc* 3C **46**
Brookfield *Lanc* 3D **33**
Brookhouse *Lanc* 4A **26**
Brookhouse *S Yor* 4B **44**
Brookhouse Green *Ches E* 2A **50**
Brookhouses *Staf* 4B **50**
Brookhurst *Mers* 4B **40**
Brooklands *G Man* 3F **41**
Brooklands *Shrp* 4D **49**
Broomedge *Warr* 4F **41**
Broomfleet *E Yor* 4E **37**
Broomhall *Ches E* 4E **49**
Broomhaugh *Nmbd* 2F **13**
Broomhill *S Yor* 2A **44**
Broomley *Nmbd* 2F **13**
Broompark *Dur* 4B **14**
Brotherlee *Dur* 1E **19**
Brothertoft *Linc* 4C **54**
Brotherton *N Yor* 4A **36**
Brotton *Red C* 3F **21**
Brough *Cumb* 3C **18**
Brough *Derbs* 4D **43**
Brough *E Yor* 4F **37**
Brough *Notts* 3E **53**
Broughall *Shrp* 4D **49**
Brougham *Cumb* 2A **18**
Brough Sowerby *Cumb* 3C **18**
Broughton *Flin* 2B **48**
Broughton *Lanc* 3D **33**
Broughton *N Lin* 2F **45**
Broughton *N Yor* 3A **30**
(nr Malton)
Broughton *N Yor* 1B **34**
(nr Skipton)
Broughton *Staf* 4F **49**
Broughton Beck *Cumb* 2D **25**
Broughton Cross *Cumb* 1B **16**
Broughton in Furness *Cumb* 2D **25**
Broughton Mills *Cumb* 1D **25**
Broughton Moor *Cumb* 1B **16**
Broughton Pk. *G Man* 2A **42**
Brown Edge *Lanc* 1B **40**
Brown Edge *Staf* 3B **50**
Brownhill *Bkbn* 3E **33**
Brownhills *Shrp* 4E **49**
Brown Knowl *Ches W* 3C **48**
Brownlow *Ches E* 2A **50**
Brownlow Heath *Ches E* 2A **50**
Broxa *N Yor* 1C **30**
Broxholme *Linc* 1F **53**
Broxton *Ches W* 3C **48**
Bruera *Ches W* 2C **48**
Brund *Staf* 2D **51**
Brunswick Village *Tyne* 1B **14**
Brunthwaite *W Yor* 2C **34**
Brunton *Nmbd* 4E **5**
Brydekirk *Dum* 1C **10**
Brymbo *Wrex* 3A **48**
Bryn *G Man* 2D **41**
Bryneglwys *Den* 4A **48**
Brynford *Flin* 1A **48**
Bryn Gates *G Man* 2D **41**
Brynteg *Wrex* 3B **48**
Bubwith *E Yor* 3D **37**
Buccleuch *Bord* 1B **6**
Buckabank *Cumb* 4E **11**
Buckden *N Yor* 3E **27**
Bucklegate *Linc* 4D **55**
Buckley *Flin* 2A **48**
Buckley Hill *Mers* 3B **40**
Bucklow Hill *Ches E* 4F **41**
Bucknall *Linc* 2B **54**
Bucknall *Stoke* 4B **50**
Buckshaw Village *Lanc* 4D **33**
Buckton *E Yor* 3E **31**
Buckton *Nmbd* 3C **4**
Buckton Vale *G Man* 2B **42**
Budby *Notts* 2C **52**
Budle *Nmbd* 3D **5**
Buerton *Ches E* 4E **49**
Buglawton *Ches E* 2A **50**
Bugthorpe *E Yor* 1D **37**
Bulcote *Notts* 4C **52**
Bulkeley *Ches E* 3D **49**
Bulmamoor *N Yor* 1C **28**
Bullbridge *Derbs* 3F **51**
Bullgill *Cumb* 1B **16**
Bulmer *N Yor* 4F **29**
Bulwell *Nott* 4B **52**
Bunbury *Ches E* 3D **49**
Bunker's Hill *Linc* 3C **54**
Burbage *Derbs* 1C **50**
Burdale *N Yor* 4B **30**
Burgh by Sands *Cumb* 3E **11**
Burgh le Marsh *Linc* 2F **55**
Burgh on Bain *Linc* 4C **46**
Burghwallis *S Yor* 1B **44**
Burland *Ches E* 3E **49**
Burley *W Yor* 3E **35**
Burleydam *Ches E* 4E **49**
Burley in Wharfedale *W Yor* 2D **35**
Burley Woodhead *W Yor* 2D **35**
Burmantofts *W Yor* 3F **35**
Burn *N Yor* 4B **36**
Burnage *G Man* 3A **42**
Burnbanks *Cumb* 3A **18**
Burnby *E Yor* 2E **37**
Burncross *S Yor* 3F **43**
Burneside *Cumb* 1A **26**
Burneston *N Yor* 2C **28**
Burnfoot *Bord* 1D **7**
(nr Hawick)
Burnfoot *Bord* 1C **6**
(nr Roberton)
Burngreave *S Yor* 4F **43**
Burnham *N Lin* 1A **46**
Burnhope *Dur* 4A **14**
Burniston *N Yor* 1D **31**
Burnlee *W Yor* 2D **43**
Burnley *Lanc* 3A **34**
Burnmouth *Bord* 1B **4**
Burn Naze *Lanc* 2B **32**
Burnopfield *Dur* 3A **14**
Burnsall *N Yor* 4F **27**
Burnt Houses *Dur* 2A **20**
Burnt Yates *N Yor* 4B **28**
Burradon *Nmbd* 2B **8**
Burradon *Tyne* 1B **14**
Burrells *Cumb* 3B **18**
Burrill *N Yor* 2B **28**
Burringham *N Lin* 2E **45**
Burscough *Lanc* 1C **40**
Burscough Bridge *Lanc* 1C **40**
Bursea *E Yor* 3E **37**
Burshill *E Yor* 2A **38**
Burslem *Stoke* 4A **50**
Burstwick *E Yor* 4C **38**
Burtersett *N Yor* 2D **27**
Burtholme *Cumb* 2A **12**
Burthwaite *Cumb* 4F **11**
Burtoft *Linc* 4C **54**
Burton *Ches W* 2D **49**
(nr Kelsall)
Burton *Ches W* 1B **48**
(nr Neston)
Burton *Nmbd* 3D **5**
Burton *Wrex* 3B **48**
Burton Agnes *E Yor* 4E **31**
Burton-by-Lincoln *Linc* 1F **53**
Burton Constable *E Yor* 3B **38**
Burton Corner *Linc* 4D **55**
Burton Fleming *E Yor* 3D **31**
Burton Green *Wrex* 3B **48**
Burton-in-Kendal *Cumb* 3A **26**
Burton in Lonsdale *N Yor* 3B **26**
Burton Joyce *Notts* 4C **52**
Burton Leonard *N Yor* 4C **28**
Burton Pedwardine *Linc* 4B **54**
Burton Pidsea *E Yor* 3C **38**
Burton Salmon *N Yor* 4A **36**
Burton Stather *N Lin* 1E **45**
Burton upon Stather *N Lin* 1E **45**
Burtonwood *Warr* 3D **41**
Burwardsley *Ches W* 3D **49**
Burwell *Linc* 1D **55**
Bury *G Man* 1A **42**
Burybank *Staf* 4A **50**
Burythorpe *N Yor* 4A **30**
Busk *Cumb* 4B **12**
Buslingthorpe *Linc* 4A **46**
Butterburn *Cumb* 1B **12**
Buttercrambe *N Yor* 1D **37**
Butterknowle *Dur* 2A **20**
Buttermere *Cumb* 3C **16**
Buttershaw *W Yor* 4D **35**
Butterton *Staf* 3C **50**
(nr Leek)
Butterton *Staf* 4A **50**
(nr Stoke-on-Trent)
Butterwick *Dur* 2C **20**
Butterwick *Linc* 4D **55**
Butterwick *N Yor* 3A **30**
(nr Malton)
Butterwick *N Yor* 3C **30**
(nr Weaverthorpe)
Butteryhaugh *Nmbd* 3E **7**
Butt Green *Ches E* 3E **49**
Butt Yeats *Lanc* 4A **26**
Buxton *Derbs* 1C **50**
Buxworth *Derbs* 4C **42**
Bwcle *Flin* 2A **48**
Bwlchgwyn *Wrex* 3A **48**
Byermoor *Tyne* 3A **14**
Byers Garth *Dur* 4C **14**
Byers Green *Dur* 1B **20**
Byker *Tyne* 2B **14**
Byland Abbey *N Yor* 3E **29**
Byley *Ches W* 2F **49**
Byram *N Yor* 4A **36**
Byrness *Nmbd* 2F **7**
Bywell *Nmbd* 2F **13**

C

Cabourne *Linc* 2B **46**
Cabus *Lanc* 2C **32**
Cadeby *S Yor* 2B **44**
Cadishead *G Man* 3F **41**
Cadley *Lanc* 3D **33**
Cadney *N Lin* 2A **46**
Cadole *Flin* 2A **48**
Caenby *Linc* 4A **46**
Caergwrle *Flin* 3B **48**
Caistor *Linc* 2B **46**
Caistron *Nmbd* 2B **8**
Calceby *Linc* 1D **55**
Caldbeck *Cumb* 1E **17**
Caldbergh *N Yor* 2F **27**
Calder Bridge *Cumb* 4B **16**
Calderbrook *G Man* 1B **42**
Calder Grove *W Yor* 1F **43**
Calder Vale *Lanc* 2D **33**
Caldwell *N Yor* 3A **20**
Caldy *Mers* 4A **40**
Calebreck *Cumb* 1E **17**
Callaly *Nmbd* 2C **8**
Calow *Derbs* 1A **52**
Calthwaite *Cumb* 4F **11**
Calton *N Yor* 1B **34**
Calton *Staf* 3D **51**
Calveley *Ches E* 3D **49**
Calver *Derbs* 1E **51**
Calverhall *Shrp* 4E **49**
Calverley *W Yor* 3E **35**
Calverton *Notts* 4C **52**
Calvo *Cumb* 3C **10**
Camblesforth *N Yor* 4C **36**
Cambo *Nmbd* 4C **8**
Cambois *Nmbd* 4F **9**
Camerton *Cumb* 1B **16**
Camerton *E Yor* 4C **38**
Cammeringham *Linc* 4F **45**
Campsall *S Yor* 1B **44**
Camptown *Bord* 1E **7**
Candlesby *Linc* 2E **55**
Canholes *Derbs* 1C **50**
Canonbie *Dum* 1E **11**
Cantley *S Yor* 2C **44**
Cantsfield *Lanc* 3B **26**
Canwick *Linc* 2F **53**
Capenhurst *Ches W* 1B **48**
Capernwray *Lanc* 3A **26**
Capheaton *Nmbd* 4C **8**
Cappercleuch *Bord* 1A **6**
Capplegill *Dum* 2A **6**
Carbrook *S Yor* 4F **43**
Carburton *Notts* 1C **52**
Car Colston *Notts* 4D **53**
Carcroft *S Yor* 2B **44**
Cardewlees *Cumb* 3E **11**
Cardurnock *Cumb* 3C **10**
Cargenbridge *Dum* 1A **10**
Cargo *Cumb* 3E **11**
Carham *Nmbd* 3A **4**
Cark *Cumb* 3E **25**
Carlbury *Darl* 3B **20**
Carlecotes *S Yor* 2D **43**
Carlesmoor *N Yor* 3A **28**
Carleton *Cumb* 3F **11**
(nr Carlisle)
Carleton *Cumb* 4B **16**
(nr Egremont)
Carleton *Cumb* 2A **18**
(nr Penrith)
Carleton *Lanc* 2B **32**
Carleton *N Yor* 2B **34**
Carleton *W Yor* 4A **36**
Carlin How *Red C* 3A **22**
Carlisle *Cumb* 3F **11** & **57**
Carlisle Lake District Airport
Cumb 2F **11**
Carlton *N Yor* 2F **29**
(nr Helmsley)
Carlton *N Yor* 2F **27**
(nr Middleham)
Carlton *N Yor* 4C **36**
(nr Selby)
Carlton *Notts* 4C **52**
Carlton *S Yor* 1F **43**
Carlton *Stoc T* 2C **20**
Carlton *W Yor* 4F **35**
Carlton Husthwaite *N Yor* 3D **29**
Carlton in Cleveland *N Yor* 4E **21**
Carlton in Lindrick *Notts* 4B **44**
Carlton-le-Moorland *Linc* 3F **53**
Carlton Miniott *N Yor* 2C **28**
Carlton-on-Trent *Notts* 2E **53**
Carlton Scroop *Linc* 4F **53**
Carmel *Flin* 1A **48**
Carnaby *E Yor* 4E **31**
Carnforth *Lanc* 3A **26**
Carperby *N Yor* 2F **27**
Carr Cross *Lanc* 1B **40**
Carrhouse *N Lin* 2D **45**
Carrington *G Man* 3F **41**
Carrington *Linc* 3D **55**
Carr Shield *Nmbd* 4D **13**
Carrutherstown *Dum* 1C **10**
Carr Vale *Derbs* 2A **52**
Carrville *Dur* 4C **14**
Carsethorn *Dum* 3A **10**
Carsington *Derbs* 3E **51**
Carterway Heads *Nmbd* 3F **13**
Carthorpe *N Yor* 2C **28**
Cartington *Nmbd* 2C **8**
Cartmel *Cumb* 3E **25**
Cartmel Fell *Cumb* 2F **25**
Cartworth *W Yor* 2D **43**
Carwath *Cumb* 4E **11**
Carwinley *Cumb* 1F **11**
Cassop *Dur* 1C **20**
Casterton *Cumb* 3B **26**
Castle Bolton *N Yor* 1F **27**
Castle Carrock *Cumb* 3A **12**
Castle Eden *Dur* 1D **21**
Castleford *W Yor* 4A **36**
Castle Heaton *Nmbd* 2B **4**
Castle O'er *Dum* 3A **6**
Castle Pk. *N Yor* 3B **22**
Castlerigg *Cumb* 2D **17**
Castleside *Dur* 4F **13**
Castleton *Derbs* 4D **43**
Castleton *G Man* 1A **42**
Castleton *N Yor* 4F **21**
Castletown *Cumb* 1A **18**
Castletown *Tyne* 3C **14**
Castley *N Yor* 2E **35**
Catchgate *Dur* 3A **14**
Catcleugh *Nmbd* 2F **7**
Catcliffe *S Yor* 4A **44**
Catforth *Lanc* 3C **32**
Catlowdy *Cumb* 1F **11**
Caton *Lanc* 4A **26**
Cattal *N Yor* 1A **36**
Catterall *Lanc* 2D **33**
Catterick *N Yor* 1B **28**
Catterick Bridge *N Yor* 1B **28**
Catterick Garrison *N Yor* 1A **28**
Catterlen *Cumb* 1F **17**
Catterton *N Yor* 2B **36**
Catton *N Yor* 3C **28**
Catton *Nmbd* 3D **13**
Catwick *E Yor* 2B **38**
Cauldmill *Bord* 1D **7**
Cauldon *Staf* 4C **50**
Cauldon Lowe *Staf* 4C **50**
Caulkerbush *Dum* 3A **10**
Caulside *Dum* 4C **6**
Caunton *Notts* 2D **53**
Causey Pk. *Nmbd* 3D **9**
Cautley *Cumb* 1B **26**
Caverswall *Staf* 4B **50**
Cawkwell *Linc* 4C **46**
Cawood *N Yor* 3B **36**
Cawthorne *N Yor* 2A **30**
Cawthorne *S Yor* 2E **43**
Cawton *N Yor* 3F **29**
Caythorpe *Linc* 4F **53**
Caythorpe *Notts* 4C **52**
Cayton *N Yor* 2D **31**
Cefn-bychan *Flin* 2A **48**
Cefn-mawr *Wrex* 4A **48**
Cefn-y-bedd *Flin* 3B **48**
Cellarhead *Staf* 4B **50**
Cessford *Bord* 1F **7**
Chadderton *G Man* 2B **42**
Chaddesden *Derb* 4F **51**
Chaddesden Common *Derb* 4F **51**
Chadwick Green *Mers* 3D **41**
Chain Bridge *Linc* 4D **55**
Chapel *Cumb* 1D **17**
Chapel Allerton *W Yor* 3E **35**
Chapel Chorlton *Staf* 4A **50**
Chapel-en-le-Frith *Derbs* 4C **42**
Chapel Haddlesey *N Yor* 4B **36**
Chapel Hill *Linc* 3C **54**
Chapelknowe *Dum* 1E **11**
Chapel-le-Dale *N Yor* 3C **26**
Chapel Milton *Derbs* 4C **42**
Chapels *Cumb* 2D **25**
Chapel St Leonards *Linc* 1F **55**
Chapel Stile *Cumb* 4E **17**
Chapelthorpe *W Yor* 1F **43**
Chapeltown *Bkbn* 1F **41**
Chapeltown *S Yor* 3F **43**
Charlesfield *Dum* 2C **10**
Charlestown *G Man* 2A **42**
Charlestown *W Yor* 4B **34**
Charlesworth *Derbs* 3C **42**
Charlton *Nmbd* 4A **8**
Charnock Green *Lanc* 1D **41**
Charnock Richard *Lanc* 1D **41**
Chatburn *Lanc* 2F **33**
Chatcull *Staf* 4F **49**
Chathill *Nmbd* 4D **5**
Chatton *Nmbd* 4C **4**
Cheadle *G Man* 4A **42**
Cheadle *Staf* 4C **50**
Cheadle Hulme *G Man* 4A **42**
Checkley *Ches E* 4F **49**
Checkley *Staf* 4C **50**
Cheddleton *Staf* 3B **50**
Cheetham Hill *G Man* 2A **42**
Chelford *Ches E* 1A **50**
Chelmorton *Derbs* 2D **51**
Chequerfield *W Yor* 4A **36**
Cherry Burton *E Yor* 2F **37**
Cherry Willingham *Linc* 1A **54**
Chesham *G Man* 1A **42**
Chester *Ches W* 2C **48** & **57**
Chesterfield *Derbs* 1F **51**
Chesterhope *Nmbd* 4A **8**
Chester-le-Street *Dur* 3B **14**
Chester Moor *Dur* 4B **14**
Chesters *Bord* 1E **7**
Chesterton *Staf* 4A **50**
Chesterwood *Nmbd* 2D **13**
Cheswick *Nmbd* 2C **4**
Chew Moor *G Man* 2E **41**
Childer Thornton *Ches W* 1B **48**
Childwall *Mers* 4C **40**
Chillingham *Nmbd* 4C **4**
Chilton *Dur* 2B **20**
Chilton Lane *Dur* 1C **20**
Chilwell *Notts* 4B **52**
Chinley *Derbs* 4C **42**
Chipping *Lanc* 2E **33**
Chirk *Wrex* 4A **48**
Chirnside *Bord* 1A **4**

Northern England Regional Atlas 67

Digmoor – Flasby

Digmoor *Lanc* 2C **40**
Dilhorne *Staf* 4B **50**
Dilston *Nmbd* 2E **13**
Dimple *G Man* 1F **41**
Dinckley *Lanc* 3E **33**
Dingle *Mers* 4B **40**
Dinnington *S Yor* 4B **44**
Dinnington *Tyne* 1B **14**
Dipton *Dur* 3A **14**
Dirt Pot *Nmbd* 4D **13**
Dishforth *N Yor* 3C **28**
Disley *Ches E* 4B **42**
Distington *Cumb* 2B **16**
Ditton *Hal* 4C **40**
Dobcross *G Man* 2B **42**
Dobs Hill *Flin* 2B **48**
Dobson's Bridge *Shrp* 4C **48**
Dockray *Cumb* 2E **17**
Doddington *Linc* 1F **53**
Doddington *Nmbd* 3B **4**
Dodleston *Ches W* 2B **48**
Dods Leigh *Staf* 4C **50**
Dodworth *S Yor* 2F **43**
Doe Lea *Derbs* 2A **52**
Dogdyke *Linc* 3C **54**
Dolphin *Flin* 1A **48**
Dolphinholme *Lanc* 1D **33**
Doncaster *S Yor* 2B **44**
Doncaster Sheffield Airport
S Yor 3C **44**
Donington *Linc* 4C **54**
Donington Eaudike *Linc* 4C **54**
Donington on Bain *Linc* 4C **46**
Donington South Ing *Linc* 4C **54**
Donna Nook *Linc* 3E **47**
Dore *S Yor* 4F **43**
Dormanstown *Red C* 2E **21**
Dornock *Dum* 2D **11**
Dorrington *Linc* 3A **54**
Dove Holes *Derbs* 1C **50**
Dovenby *Cumb* 1B **16**
Doveridge *Derbs* 4D **51**
Dowbridge *Lanc* 3C **32**
Downall Green *Mers* 2D **41**
Downham *Lanc* 2F **33**
Downham *Nmbd* 3A **4**
Downholland Cross *Lanc* 2B **40**
Downholme *N Yor* 1A **28**
Dowthwaitehead *Cumb* 2E **17**
Doxford *Nmbd* 4D **5**
Dragonby *N Lin* 1F **45**
Draughton *N Yor* 1C **34**
Drax *N Yor* 4C **36**
Draycott in the Moors *Staf* 4B **50**
Drayton *Linc* 4C **54**
Drebley *N Yor* 1C **34**
Driby *Linc* 1D **55**
Driffield *E Yor* 1A **38**
Drigg *Cumb* 1B **24**
Drighlington *W Yor* 4E **35**
Dringhoe *E Yor* 1B **38**
Dronfield *Derbs* 1F **51**
Dronfield Woodhouse *Derbs* 1F **51**
Droylsden *G Man* 3A **42**
Drumburgh *Cumb* 3D **11**
Drumburn *Dum* 2A **10**
Drumsleet *Dum* 1A **10**
Drury *Flin* 2A **48**
Drybeck *Cumb* 3B **18**
Dry Doddington *Linc* 4E **53**
Duckington *Ches W* 3C **48**
Duckmanton *Derbs* 1A **52**
Duddo *Nmbd* 2B **4**
Duddon *Ches W* 2D **49**
Duddon Bridge *Cumb* 2C **24**
Dudleston *Shrp* 4B **48**
Dudleston Heath *Shrp* 4B **48**
Dudley *Tyne* 1B **14**
Duffield *Derbs* 4F **51**
Dufton *Cumb* 2B **18**
Duggleby *N Yor* 4B **30**
Dukesfield *Nmbd* 3E **13**
Dukinfield *G Man* 3B **42**
Dumfries *Dum* 1A **10** & **57**
Duncow *Dum* 1A **10**
Dundraw *Cumb* 4D **11**
Dunford Bridge *S Yor* 2D **43**
Dungworth *S Yor* 4E **43**
Dunham-on-the-Hill *Ches W* 1C **48**
Dunham-on-Trent *Notts* 1E **53**
Dunham Town *G Man* 4F **41**
Dunham Woodhouses *G Man* 4F **41**
Dunholme *Linc* 1A **54**
Dunkeswick *N Yor* 2F **35**
Dunkirk *Staf* 3A **50**
Dunnington *E Yor* 1B **38**
Dunnington *York* 1C **36**
Dunningwell *Cumb* 2C **24**
Dunnockshaw *Lanc* 4A **34**
Duns *Bord* 1A **4**
Dunscar *G Man* 1F **41**
Dunscore *Dum* 1A **10**
Dunscroft *S Yor* 2C **44**
Dunsdale *Red C* 3F **21**
Dunsley *N Yor* 3B **22**
Dunsop Bridge *Lanc* 1E **33**
Dunstan *Nmbd* 1E **9**
Dunston *Linc* 2A **54**
Dunston *Tyne* 2B **14**
Dunsville *S Yor* 2C **44**
Dunswell *E Yor* 3A **38**
Dunwood *Staf* 3B **50**
Durdar *Cumb* 3F **11**
Durham *Dur* 4B **14** & **58**
Durham Tees Valley Airport
Darl 3C **20**
Durkar *W Yor* 1F **43**
Dutton *Ches W* 1D **49**
Dykesfield *Cumb* 3E **11**

E

Eachwick *Nmbd* 1A **14**
Eagland Hill *Lanc* 2C **32**
Eagle *Linc* 2E **53**
Eagle Barnsdale *Linc* 2E **53**
Eagle Moor *Linc* 2E **53**
Eaglescliffe *Stoc T* 3D **21**
Eaglesfield *Cumb* 2B **16**
Eaglesfield *Dum* 1D **11**
Eagley *G Man* 1F **41**
Eakring *Notts* 2C **52**
Ealand *N Lin* 1D **45**
Eals *Nmbd* 3B **12**
Eamont Bridge *Cumb* 2A **18**
Earby *Lanc* 2B **34**
Earcroft *Bkbn* 4E **33**
Earle *Nmbd* 4B **4**
Earlesfield *Linc* 4F **53**
Earlestown *Mers* 3D **41**
Earlsheaton *W Yor* 4E **35**
Earl Sterndale *Derbs* 2C **50**
Earsdon *Tyne* 1C **14**
Earswick *York* 1C **36**
Easby *N Yor* 4E **21**
(nr Great Ayton)
Easby *N Yor* 4A **20**
(nr Richmond)
Easington *Dur* 4D **15**
Easington *E Yor* 1D **47**
Easington *Nmbd* 3D **5**
Easington *Red C* 3A **22**
Easington Colliery *Dur* 4D **15**
Easington Lane *Tyne* 4C **14**
Easingwold *N Yor* 3E **29**
East Appleton *N Yor* 1B **28**
East Ardsley *W Yor* 4F **35**
East Ayton *N Yor* 2C **30**
East Barkwith *Linc* 4B **46**
East Barnby *N Yor* 3B **22**
East Bierley *W Yor* 4E **35**
East Bolton *Nmbd* 1D **9**
Eastbourne *Darl* 3B **20**
East Bridgford *Notts* 4C **52**
East Briscoe *Dur* 3E **19**
Eastburn *W Yor* 2C **34**
East Butsfield *Dur* 4A **14**
East Butterwick *N Lin* 2E **45**
Eastby *N Yor* 1C **34**
East Carlton *W Yor* 2E **35**
East Common *N Yor* 3C **36**
East Cottingwith *E Yor* 2D **37**
East Cowick *E Yor* 4C **36**
East Cowton *N Yor* 4C **20**
East Cramlington *Nmbd* 1B **14**
East Drayton *Notts* 1D **53**
East Ella *Hull* 4A **38**
East End *E Yor* 1B **38**
(nr Ulrome)
East End *E Yor* 4C **38**
(nr Withernsea)
East Ferry *Linc* 3E **45**
Eastfield *N Yor* 2D **31**
Eastfield Hall *Nmbd* 2E **9**
East Garforth *W Yor* 3A **36**
Eastgate *Dur* 1E **19**
East Halton *N Lin* 4B **38**
Eastham *Mers* 4B **40**
Eastham Ferry *Mers* 4B **40**
East Hardwick *W Yor* 1A **44**
East Harlsey *N Yor* 1D **29**
East Hartford *Nmbd* 1B **14**
East Hauxwell *N Yor* 1A **28**
East Heckington *Linc* 4B **54**
East Hedleyhope *Dur* 4A **14**
East Heslerton *N Yor* 3C **30**
Easthorpe *Leics* 4E **53**
East Horton *Nmbd* 3C **4**
East Keal *Linc* 2D **55**
East Keswick *W Yor* 2F **35**
East Kirkby *Linc* 2D **55**
East Knapton *N Yor* 3B **30**
East Kyloe *Nmbd* 3C **4**
East Layton *N Yor* 4A **20**
East Learmouth *Nmbd* 3A **4**
East Lilburn *Nmbd* 4C **4**
East Lound *N Lin* 3D **45**
East Lutton *N Yor* 4C **30**
East Markham *Notts* 1D **53**
East Marton *N Yor* 1B **34**
East Morton *W Yor* 2D **35**
East Ness *N Yor* 3F **29**
East Newton *E Yor* 3C **38**
East Newton *N Yor* 3F **29**
Eastoft *N Lin* 1E **45**
Easton *Cumb* 3D **11**
(nr Burgh by Sands)
Easton *Cumb* 1F **11**
(nr Longtown)
East Ord *Nmbd* 1B **4**
East Rainton *Tyne* 4C **14**
East Ravendale *NE Lin* 3C **46**
Eastriggs *Dum* 2D **11**
East Rigton *W Yor* 2F **35**
Eastrington *E Yor* 4D **37**
East Rounton *N Yor* 4D **21**
East Row *N Yor* 3B **22**
East Shaws *Dur* 3F **19**
East Sleekburn *Nmbd* 4E **9**
East Stockwith *Linc* 3D **45**
East Stoke *Notts* 4D **53**
East Thirston *Nmbd* 3D **9**
East Torrington *Linc* 4B **46**
Eastville *Linc* 3E **55**
East Witton *N Yor* 2A **28**
Eastwood *Notts* 4A **52**
East Woodburn *Nmbd* 4B **8**
Eaton *Ches E* 2A **50**
Eaton *Ches W* 2D **49**
Eaton *Notts* 1D **53**
Ebberston *N Yor* 2B **30**
Ebchester *Dur* 3A **14**
Ebnal *Ches W* 4C **48**
Ecclefechan *Dum* 1C **10**
Eccles *Bord* 2A **4**
Eccles *G Man* 3F **41**
Ecclesall *S Yor* 4F **43**
Ecclesfield *S Yor* 3F **43**
Eccleshill *W Yor* 3D **35**
Eccleston *Ches W* 2C **48**
Eccleston *Lanc* 1D **41**
Eccleston *Mers* 3C **40**
Eccup *W Yor* 2E **35**
Eckford *Bord* 1F **7**
Eckington *Derbs* 1A **52**
Edale *Derbs* 4D **43**
Edderside *Cumb* 4C **10**
Edenfield *Lanc* 1F **41**
Edenhall *Cumb* 1A **18**
Edensor *Derbs* 1E **51**
Edenthorpe *S Yor* 2C **44**
Eden Vale *Dur* 1D **21**
Edge Green *Ches W* 3C **48**
Edgeley *Shrp* 4D **49**
Edgeside *Lanc* 4A **34**
Edgworth *Bkbn* 1F **41**
Edingley *Notts* 3C **52**
Edlaston *Derbs* 4D **51**
Edlingham *Nmbd* 2D **9**
Edlington *Linc* 1C **54**
Edmondsley *Dur* 4B **14**
Edmundbyers *Dur* 3F **13**
Ednaston *Derbs* 4E **51**
Edrom *Bord* 1A **4**
Edwalton *Notts* 4B **52**
Edwinstowe *Notts* 2C **52**
Egerton *G Man* 1F **41**
Eggborough *N Yor* 4B **36**
Egglescliffe *Stoc T* 3D **21**
Eggleston *Dur* 2E **19**
Eglingham *Nmbd* 1D **9**
Egmanton *Notts* 2D **53**
Egremont *Cumb* 3B **16**
Egremont *Mers* 3B **40**
Egton *N Yor* 4B **22**
Egton Bridge *N Yor* 4B **22**
Eldon *Dur* 2B **20**
Eldroth *N Yor* 4C **26**
Eldwick *W Yor* 2D **35**
Elfhowe *Cumb* 1F **25**
Elford *Nmbd* 3D **5**
Elishaw *Nmbd* 3A **8**
Elizafield *Dum* 1B **10**
Elkesley *Notts* 1C **52**
Elland *W Yor* 4D **35**
Ellastone *Staf* 4D **51**
Ellel *Lanc* 1C **32**
Ellenborough *Cumb* 1B **16**
Ellerbeck *N Yor* 1D **29**
Ellerburn *N Yor* 2B **30**
Ellerby *N Yor* 3A **22**
Ellerker *E Yor* 4F **37**
Ellerton *E Yor* 3D **37**
Ellerton-on-Swale *N Yor* 1B **28**
Ellesmere *Shrp* 4C **48**
Ellesmere Port *Ches W* 1C **48**
Ellingham *Nmbd* 4D **5**
Ellingstring *N Yor* 2A **28**
Ellington *Nmbd* 3E **9**
Ellonby *Cumb* 1F **17**
Elloughton *E Yor* 4F **37**
Elmswell *E Yor* 1F **37**
Elmton *Derbs* 1B **52**
Elsdon *Nmbd* 3B **8**
Elsecar *S Yor* 3F **43**
Elsham *N Lin* 1A **46**
Elslack *N Yor* 2B **34**
Elstob *Dur* 2C **20**
Elston *Lanc* 3E **33**
Elston *Notts* 4D **53**
Elstronwick *E Yor* 3C **38**
Elswick *Lanc* 3C **32**
Elswick *Tyne* 2B **14**
Elterwater *Cumb* 4E **17**
Elton *Ches W* 1C **48**
Elton *Derbs* 2E **51**
Elton *G Man* 1F **41**
Elton *Notts* 4D **53**
Elton *Stoc T* 3D **21**
Elton Green *Ches W* 1C **48**
Eltringham *Nmbd* 2F **13**
Elvington *York* 2D **37**
Elwick *Hart* 1D **21**
Elwick *Nmbd* 3D **5**
Elworth *Ches E* 2F **49**
Embleton *Cumb* 1C **16**
Embleton *Hart* 2D **21**
Embleton *Nmbd* 4E **5**
Embsay *N Yor* 1C **34**
Emley *W Yor* 1E **43**
Endmoor *Cumb* 2A **26**
Endon *Staf* 3B **50**
Endon Bank *Staf* 3B **50**
Englesea-brook *Ches E* 3F **49**
Ennerdale Bridge *Cumb* 3B **16**
Epperstone *Notts* 4C **52**
Eppleby *N Yor* 3A **20**
Eppleworth *E Yor* 3A **38**
Epworth *N Lin* 2D **45**
Epworth Turbary *N Lin* 2D **45**
Erbistock *Wrex* 4B **48**
Ermine *Linc* 1F **53**
Eryholme *N Yor* 4C **20**
Eryrys *Den* 3A **48**
Escomb *Dur* 1A **20**
Escrick *N Yor* 2C **36**
Esh *Dur* 4A **14**
Esholt *W Yor* 2D **35**
Eshott *Nmbd* 3E **9**
Eshton *N Yor* 1B **34**
Esh Winning *Dur* 4A **14**
Eskdale Green *Cumb* 4C **16**
Eskdalemuir *Dum* 3A **6**
Eskham *Linc* 3D **47**
Esk Valley *N Yor* 4B **22**
Eslington Hall *Nmbd* 1C **8**
Esprick *Lanc* 3C **32**
Eston *Red C* 3E **21**
Etal *Nmbd* 3B **4**
Etherley Dene *Dur* 2A **20**
Ettersgill *Dur* 2D **19**
Ettiley Heath *Ches E* 2F **49**
Etton *E Yor* 2F **37**
Ettrick *Bord* 1A **6**
Ettrickbridge *Bord* 1B **6**
Euxton *Lanc* 1D **41**
Evedon *Linc* 4A **54**
Evenwood *Dur* 2A **20**
Evenwood Gate *Dur* 2A **20**
Everingham *E Yor* 2E **37**
Everley *N Yor* 2C **30**
Everthorpe *E Yor* 3F **37**
Everton *Mers* 3B **40**
Everton *Notts* 3C **44**
Evertown *Dum* 1E **11**
Ewden Village *S Yor* 3E **43**
Ewerby *Linc* 4B **54**
Ewes *Dum* 3B **6**
Ewesley *Nmbd* 3C **8**
Ewlo *Flin* 2A **48**
Ewloe *Flin* 2A **48**
Ewood Bridge *Lanc* 4F **33**
Exelby *N Yor* 2B **28**
Eyam *Derbs* 1E **51**
Eyemouth *Bord* 1B **4**
Eyton *Wrex* 4B **48**

F

Faceby *N Yor* 4D **21**
Faddiley *Ches E* 3D **49**
Fadmoor *N Yor* 2F **29**
Failsworth *G Man* 2B **42**
Fairburn *N Yor* 4A **36**
Fairfield *Derbs* 1C **50**
Fair Hill *Cumb* 1A **18**
Faldingworth *Linc* 4A **46**
Fallowfield *G Man* 3A **42**
Falsgrave *N Yor* 2D **31**
Falstone *Nmbd* 4F **7**
Fangdale Beck *N Yor* 1E **29**
Fangfoss *E Yor* 1D **37**
Farforth *Linc* 1D **55**
Farington *Lanc* 4D **33**
Farlam *Cumb* 3A **12**
Farlesthorpe *Linc* 1E **55**
Farleton *Cumb* 2A **26**
Farleton *Lanc* 4A **26**
Farley *Staf* 4C **50**
Farlington *N Yor* 4F **29**
Far Moor *G Man* 2D **41**
Farnah Green *Derbs* 4F **51**
Farndon *Ches W* 3C **48**
Farndon *Notts* 3D **53**
Farnham *N Yor* 4C **28**
Farnhill *N Yor* 2C **34**
Farnley *N Yor* 2E **35**
Farnley Tyas *W Yor* 1D **43**
Farnsfield *Notts* 3C **52**
Farnworth *G Man* 2F **41**
Farnworth *Hal* 4D **41**
Far Sawrey *Cumb* 1E **25**
Farsley *W Yor* 3E **35**
Farthorpe *Linc* 1C **54**
Fartown *W Yor* 1D **43**
Fatfield *Tyne* 3C **14**
Faugh *Cumb* 3A **12**
Faverdale *Darl* 3B **20**
Fawdington *N Yor* 3D **29**
Fawfieldhead *Staf* 2C **50**
Faxfleet *E Yor* 4E **37**
Fazakerley *Mers* 3B **40**
Fearby *N Yor* 2A **28**
Fearnhead *Warr* 3E **41**
Featherstone *W Yor* 4A **36**
Featherstone Castle *Nmbd* 2B **12**
Feetham *N Yor* 1E **27**
Feizor *N Yor* 4C **26**
Felixkirk *N Yor* 2D **29**
Felkington *Nmbd* 2B **4**
Fell End *Cumb* 1C **26**
Felling *Tyne* 2B **14**
Fell Side *Cumb* 1E **17**
Felton *Nmbd* 2D **9**
Fenay Bridge *W Yor* 1D **43**
Fence *Lanc* 3A **34**
Fence Houses *Tyne* 3C **14**
Fenham *Nmbd* 2C **4**
Fenham *Tyne* 2B **14**
Fenhouses *Linc* 4C **54**
Feniscowles *Bkbn* 4E **33**
Fenn's Bank *Wrex* 4D **49**
Fenny Bentley *Derbs* 3D **51**
Fenrother *Nmbd* 3D **9**
Fenton *Cumb* 3A **12**
Fenton *Linc* 3E **53**
(nr Caythorpe)
Fenton *Linc* 1E **53**
(nr Saxilby)
Fenton *Nmbd* 3B **4**
Fenton *Notts* 4D **45**
Fenton *Stoke* 4A **50**
Fenwick *Nmbd* 2C **4**
(nr Berwick-upon-Tweed)
Fenwick *Nmbd* 1F **13**
(nr Hexham)
Fenwick *S Yor* 1B **44**
Fernilee *Derbs* 1C **50**
Ferrensby *N Yor* 4C **28**
Ferriby Sluice *N Lin* 4F **37**
Ferrybridge *W Yor* 4A **36**
Ferryhill *Dur* 1B **20**
Ferryhill Station *Dur* 1C **20**
Fewston *N Yor* 1D **35**
Y Fflint *Flin* 1A **48**
Ffrith *Flin* 3A **48**
Field Broughton *Cumb* 2E **25**
Fieldhead *Cumb* 1F **17**
Filey *N Yor* 2E **31**
Fillingham *Linc* 4F **45**
Fimber *E Yor* 4B **30**
Finghall *N Yor* 2A **28**
Fingland *Cumb* 3D **11**
Finningley *S Yor* 3C **44**
Finsthwaite *Cumb* 2E **25**
Firbeck *S Yor* 4B **44**
Firby *N Yor* 2B **28**
(nr Bedale)
Firby *N Yor* 4A **30**
(nr Malton)
Firgrove *G Man* 1B **42**
Firsby *Linc* 2E **55**
Fir Tree *Dur* 1A **20**
Fishburn *Dur* 1C **20**
Fisher's Row *Lanc* 2C **32**
Fishlake *S Yor* 1C **44**
Fishpool *G Man* 1A **42**
Fishtoft *Linc* 4D **55**
Fishtoft Drove *Linc* 4D **55**
Fishwick *Bord* 1B **4**
Fiskerton *Linc* 1A **54**
Fiskerton *Notts* 3D **53**
Fitling *E Yor* 3C **38**
Fitzwilliam *W Yor* 1A **44**
Flagg *Derbs* 2D **51**
Flamborough *E Yor* 3F **31**
Flasby *N Yor* 1B **34**

Northern England Regional Atlas 69

Flash – Hall Green

Flash *Staf* 2C 50
Flatt, The *Cumb* 1A 12
Flawborough *Notts* 4D 53
Flawith *N Yor* 4D 29
Flaxby *N Yor* 1F 35
Flaxholme *Derbs* 4F 51
Flaxton *N Yor* 4F 29
Fledborough *Notts* 1E 53
Fleetwood *Lanc* 2B 32
Fletchertown *Cumb* 4D 11
Flimby *Cumb* 1B 16
Flint *Flin* 1A 48
Flintham *Notts* 4D 53
Flint Mountain *Flin* 1A 48
Flinton *E Yor* 3C 38
Flixborough *N Lin* 1E 45
Flixton *G Man* 3F 41
Flixton *N Yor* 3D 31
Flockton *W Yor* 1E 43
Flodden *Nmbd* 3B 4
Flookburgh *Cumb* 3E 25
Flotterton *Nmbd* 2B 8
Fockerby *N Lin* 1E 45
Foggathorpe *E Yor* 3D 37
Fogo *Bord* 2A 4
Fogorig *Bord* 2A 4
Fole *Staf* 4C 50
Folkingham *Linc* 4A 54
Folkton *N Yor* 3D 31
Follifoot *N Yor* 1F 35
Foolow *Derbs* 1D 51
Force Forge *Cumb* 1E 25
Force Mills *Cumb* 1E 25
Forcett *N Yor* 3A 20
Ford *Derbs* 4A 44
Ford *Nmbd* 3B 4
Ford *Staf* 3C 50
Ford Green *Lanc* 2C 32
Fordington *Linc* 1E 55
Fordon *E Yor* 3D 31
Forest *N Yor* 4B 20
Forestburn Gate *Nmbd* 3C 8
Forest Hall *Cumb* 4A 18
Forest Head *Cumb* 3A 12
Forest-in-Teesdale *Dur* 2D 19
Forest Town *Notts* 2B 52
Formby *Mers* 2B 40
Forsbrook *Staf* 4B 50
Forton *Lanc* 1C 32
Foston *Linc* 4E 53
Foston *N Yor* 4F 29
Foston on the Wolds *E Yor* 1B 38
Fotherby *Linc* 3D 47
Fothergill *Cumb* 1B 16
Foulbridge *Cumb* 4F 11
Foulden *Bord* 1B 4
Foulridge *Lanc* 2A 34
Four Lane End *S Yor* 2E 43
Four Lane Ends *Lanc* 1D 33
Fourlanes End *Ches E* 3A 50
Fourstones *Nmbd* 2D 13
Fowley Common *Warr* 3E 41
Foxfield *Cumb* 2D 25
Foxholes *N Yor* 3D 31
Foxt *Staf* 4C 50
Foxton *Dur* 2C 20
Foxton *N Yor* 1D 29
Foxup *N Yor* 3D 27
Foxwist Green *Ches W* 2E 49
Fraisthorpe *E Yor* 4E 31
Frampton *Linc* 4D 55
Frampton West End *Linc* 4C 54
Framwellgate Moor *Dur* 4B 14
Frandley *Ches W* 1E 49
Frankby *Mers* 4A 40
Freckleton *Lanc* 4C 32
Freehay *Staf* 4C 50
Freiston *Linc* 4D 55
Freiston Shore *Linc* 4D 55
Fremington *N Yor* 1F 27
Freshfield *Mers* 2A 40
Fridaythorpe *E Yor* 1E 37
Friden *Derbs* 2D 51
Friesthorpe *Linc* 4A 46
Frieston *Linc* 4F 53
Friezeland *Notts* 3A 52
Friskney *Linc* 3E 55
Friskney Eaudyke *Linc* 3E 55
Fritchley *Derbs* 3F 51
Frith Bank *Linc* 4D 55
Frithville *Linc* 3D 55
Frizinghall *W Yor* 3D 35
Frizington *Cumb* 3B 16
Frodingham *N Lin* 1F 45
Frodsham *Ches W* 1D 49
Froggatt *Derbs* 1E 51
Froghall *Staf* 4C 50
Froncysyllte *Wrex* 4A 48
Fron Isaf *Wrex* 4A 48
Frosterley *Dur* 1F 19
Fryton *N Yor* 3F 29
Fulbeck *Linc* 3F 53
Fulford *Staf* 4B 50
Fulford *York* 2C 36
Fuller's Moor *Ches W* 3C 48
Fulletby *Linc* 1C 54
Full Sutton *E Yor* 1D 37
Fulnetby *Linc* 1A 54
Fulstow *Linc* 3D 47
Fulthorpe *Stoc T* 2D 21
Fulwell *Tyne* 3C 14
Fulwood *Lanc* 3D 33
Fulwood *Notts* 3A 52
Fulwood *S Yor* 4E 43
Furness Vale *Derbs* 4C 42
Fylingthorpe *N Yor* 4C 22

G

Gainford *Dur* 3A 20
Gainsborough *Linc* 3E 45
Gaisgill *Cumb* 4B 18
Gaitsgill *Cumb* 4E 11
Galgate *Lanc* 1C 32
Gallows Green *Staf* 4C 50
Galphay *N Yor* 3B 28
Gamblesby *Cumb* 1B 18
Gamelsby *Cumb* 3D 11
Gamesley *Derbs* 3C 42
Gammersgill *N Yor* 2F 27
Gamston *Notts* 4C 52
(nr Nottingham)
Gamston *Notts* 1D 53
(nr Retford)
Ganstead *E Yor* 3B 38
Ganthorpe *N Yor* 3F 29
Ganton *N Yor* 3C 30
Garden City *Flin* 2B 48
Garden Village *S Yor* 3E 43
Gardham *E Yor* 2F 37
Garforth *W Yor* 3A 36
Gargrave *N Yor* 1B 34
Garmondsway *Dur* 1C 20
Garnett Bridge *Cumb* 1A 26
Garrigill *Cumb* 4C 12
Garriston *N Yor* 1A 28
Garsdale *Cumb* 2C 26
Garsdale Head *Cumb* 1C 26
Garshall Green *Staf* 4B 50
Garstang *Lanc* 2C 32
Garston *Mers* 4C 40
Garswood *Mers* 3D 41
Garth *Wrex* 4A 48
Garthorpe *N Lin* 1E 45
Garth Row *Cumb* 1A 26
Garton *E Yor* 3C 38
Garton-on-the-Wolds *E Yor* 1F 37
Garwick *Linc* 4B 54
Gateacre *Mers* 4C 40
Gatebeck *Cumb* 2A 26
Gate Burton *Linc* 4E 45
Gateforth *N Yor* 4B 36
Gate Helmsley *N Yor* 1C 36
Gatehouse *Nmbd* 4F 7
Gatenby *N Yor* 2C 28
Gatesgarth *Cumb* 3C 16
Gateshead *Tyne* 2B 14
Gatesheath *Ches W* 2C 48
Gathurst *G Man* 2D 41
Gatley *G Man* 4A 42
Gautby *Linc* 1B 54
Gavinton *Bord* 1A 4
Gawber *S Yor* 2F 43
Gawsworth *Ches E* 2A 50
Gawthorpe *W Yor* 4E 35
Gawthrop *Cumb* 2B 26
Gawthwaite *Cumb* 2D 25
Gayle *N Yor* 2D 27
Gayles *N Yor* 4A 20
Gayton *Mers* 4A 40
Gayton le Marsh *Linc* 4E 47
Gayton le Wold *Linc* 4C 46
Gedling *Notts* 4C 52
Gee Cross *G Man* 3B 42
Gelston *Linc* 4F 53
Gembling *E Yor* 1B 38
Gerrard's Bromley *Staf* 4F 49
Gibraltar *Linc* 3F 55
Gibsmere *Notts* 4D 53
Giggleswick *N Yor* 4D 27
Gilberdyke *E Yor* 4E 37
Gilcrux *Cumb* 1C 16
Gildersome *W Yor* 4E 35
Gildingwells *S Yor* 4B 44
Gilesgate Moor *Dur* 4B 14
Gilgarran *Cumb* 2B 16
Gillamoor *N Yor* 1F 29
Gillar's Green *Mers* 3C 40
Gilling East *N Yor* 3F 29
Gilling West *N Yor* 4A 20
Gillow Heath *Staf* 3A 50
Gilmanscleuch *Bord* 1B 6
Gilmonby *Dur* 3E 19
Gilsland *Nmbd* 2B 12
Gilsland Spa *Cumb* 2B 12
Giltbrook *Notts* 4A 52
Gipsey Bridge *Linc* 4C 54
Gipton *W Yor* 3F 35
Girsby *N Yor* 4C 20
Girton *Notts* 2E 53
Gisburn *Lanc* 2A 34
Glaisdale *N Yor* 4A 22
Glanton *Nmbd* 1C 8
Glanton Pyke *Nmbd* 1C 8
Glan-y-don *Flin* 1A 48
Glapwell *Derbs* 2A 52
Glasshouses *N Yor* 4A 28
Glasson *Cumb* 2D 11
Glasson *Lanc* 1C 32
Glassonby *Cumb* 1A 18
Glazebrook *Warr* 3E 41
Glazebury *Warr* 3E 41
Gleadless *S Yor* 4F 43
Gleadsmoss *Ches E* 2A 50
Gleaston *Cumb* 3D 25
Gledrid *Shrp* 4A 48
Glencaple *Dum* 2A 10
Glenkerry *Bord* 1A 6
Glenkiln *Dum* 1A 10
Glenridding *Cumb* 3E 17
Glentham *Linc* 3A 46
Glentworth *Linc* 4F 45
Glenzierfoot *Dum* 1E 11
Glossop *Derbs* 3C 42
Gloster Hill *Nmbd* 2E 9
Glusburn *N Yor* 2C 34
Glutton Bridge *Derbs* 2C 50
Glyn Ceiriog *Wrex* 4A 48
Glyndyfrdwy *Den* 4A 48
Goathland *N Yor* 4B 22
Gobowen *Shrp* 4B 48
Godleybrook *Staf* 4B 50
Godstone *Staf* 4C 50
Golborne *G Man* 3E 41
Golcar *W Yor* 1C 42
Golden Grove *N Yor* 4B 22
Goldenhill *Stoke* 3A 50
Goldsborough *N Yor* 1F 35
(nr Harrogate)
Goldsborough *N Yor* 3B 22
(nr Whitby)
Goldthorpe *S Yor* 2A 44
Gollinglith Foot *N Yor* 2A 28
Gomersal *W Yor* 4E 35
Gonalston *Notts* 4C 52
Gonerby Hill Foot *Linc* 4F 53
Goodmanham *E Yor* 2E 37
Goodshaw *Lanc* 4A 34
Goodshaw Fold *Lanc* 4A 34
Goole *E Yor* 4D 37
Goose Green *Cumb* 2A 26
Goosnargh *Lanc* 3D 33
Goostrey *Ches E* 1F 49
Gorsedd *Flin* 1A 48
Gorseybank *Derbs* 3E 51
Gorstella *Ches W* 2B 48
Gorton *G Man* 3A 42
Gosforth *Cumb* 4B 16
Gosforth *Tyne* 2B 14
Goswick *Nmbd* 2C 4
Goulceby *Linc* 1C 54
Goverton *Notts* 4D 53
Gowdall *E Yor* 4C 36
Gowthorpe *E Yor* 1D 37
Goxhill *E Yor* 2B 38
Goxhill *N Lin* 4B 38
Goxhill Haven *N Lin* 4B 38
Grafton *N Yor* 4D 29
Graianrhyd *Den* 3A 48
Graig-fechan *Den* 3A 48
Grainsby *Linc* 3C 46
Grainthorpe *Linc* 3D 47
Grainthorpe Fen *Linc* 3D 47
Graiselound *N Lin* 3D 45
Granby *Notts* 4D 53
Grange *Cumb* 3D 17
Grange *Mers* 4A 40
Grange, The *N Yor* 1E 29
Grangemill *Derbs* 3E 51
Grange Moor *W Yor* 1E 43
Grange-over-Sands *Cumb* 3F 25
Grangetown *Red C* 2E 21
Grange Villa *Dur* 3B 14
Gransmoor *E Yor* 1B 38
Grantham *Linc* 4F 53
Grantley *N Yor* 4B 28
Grantshouse *Bord* 1A 4
Grappenhall *Warr* 4E 41
Grasby *Linc* 2A 46
Grasmere *Cumb* 4E 17
Grasscroft *G Man* 2B 42
Grassendale *Mers* 4B 40
Grassgarth *Cumb* 4E 11
Grassholme *Dur* 2E 19
Grassington *N Yor* 4F 27
Grassmoor *Derbs* 2A 52
Grassthorpe *Notts* 2D 53
Gratton *Staf* 3B 50
Gravel Hole *G Man* 2B 42
Grayingham *Linc* 3F 45
Grayrigg *Cumb* 1A 26
Grayson Green *Cumb* 2A 16
Graythorp *Hart* 2E 21
Greasbrough *S Yor* 3A 44
Greasby *Mers* 4A 40
Great Altcar *Lanc* 2B 40
Great Asby *Cumb* 3B 18
Great Ayton *N Yor* 3E 21
Great Barrow *Ches W* 2C 48
Great Barugh *N Yor* 3A 30
Great Bavington *Nmbd* 4B 8
Great Blencow *Cumb* 1F 17
Great Broughton *Cumb* 1B 16
Great Broughton *N Yor* 4E 21
Great Budworth *Ches W* 1E 49
Great Burdon *Darl* 3C 20
Great Busby *N Yor* 4E 21
Great Carlton *Linc* 4E 47
Great Chilton *Dur* 1B 20
Great Cliff *W Yor* 1F 43
Great Clifton *Cumb* 2B 16
Great Coates *NE Lin* 1C 46
Great Corby *Cumb* 3F 11
Great Cowden *E Yor* 2C 38
Great Crakehall *N Yor* 1B 28
Great Crosby *Mers* 2B 40
Great Cubley *Derbs* 4D 51
Great Eccleston *Lanc* 2C 32
Great Edstone *N Yor* 2A 30
Great Eppleton *Tyne* 4C 14
Great Fencote *N Yor* 1B 28
Great Gate *Staf* 4C 50
Great Givendale *E Yor* 1E 37
Great Gonerby *Linc* 4E 53
Great Habton *N Yor* 3A 30
Great Hale *Linc* 4B 54
Greatham *Hart* 2D 21
Great Harwood *Lanc* 3F 33
Great Hatfield *E Yor* 2B 38
Great Heck *N Yor* 4B 36
Great Horton *W Yor* 3D 35
Great Houghton *S Yor* 2A 44
Great Hucklow *Derbs* 1D 51
Great Kelk *E Yor* 1B 38
Great Kendale *E Yor* 4D 31
Great Langdale *Cumb* 4D 17
Great Langton *N Yor* 1B 28
Great Limber *Linc* 2B 46
Great Longstone *Derbs* 1E 51
Great Lumley *Dur* 4B 14
Great Marton *Bkpl* 3B 32
Great Mitton *Lanc* 3F 33
Great Musgrave *Cumb* 3C 18
Great Ormside *Cumb* 3C 18
Great Orton *Cumb* 3E 11
Great Ouseburn *N Yor* 4D 29
Great Plumpton *Lanc* 3B 32
Great Preston *W Yor* 4A 36
Great Ryle *Nmbd* 1C 8
Great Salkeld *Cumb* 1A 18
Great Sankey *Warr* 4D 41
Great Smeaton *N Yor* 4C 20
Great Stainton *Darl* 2C 20
Great Steeping *Linc* 2E 55
Great Strickland *Cumb* 2A 18
Great Sturton *Linc* 1C 54
Great Sutton *Ches W* 1B 48
Great Swinburne *Nmbd* 1E 13
Great Thirkleby *N Yor* 3D 29
Great Tosson *Nmbd* 2C 8
Great Tows *Linc* 3C 46
Great Urswick *Cumb* 3D 25
Great Whittington *Nmbd* 1F 13
Grebby *Linc* 2E 55
Green, The *Cumb* 2C 24
Greencroft *Dur* 3A 14
Greendykes *Nmbd* 4C 4
Green End *N Yor* 4B 22
Greenfield *Flin* 1A 48
Greenfield *G Man* 2B 42
Greengill *Cumb* 1C 16
Greenhalgh *Lanc* 3C 32
Green Hammerton *N Yor* 1A 36
Greenhaugh *Nmbd* 4F 7
Greenhead *Nmbd* 2B 12
Greenhill *Dum* 1C 10
Greenhill *S Yor* 4F 43
Greenhow Hill *N Yor* 4A 28
Greenlea *Dum* 1B 10
Greenmount *G Man* 1F 41
Greenodd *Cumb* 2E 25
Greenrow *Cumb* 3C 10
Greenside *Tyne* 2A 14
Greensidehill *Nmbd* 1B 8
Greenwell *Cumb* 3A 12
Greetham *Linc* 1D 55
Greetland *W Yor* 4C 34
Gregson Lane *Lanc* 4D 33
Grenoside *S Yor* 3F 43
Gresford *Wrex* 3B 48
Gressingham *Lanc* 4A 26
Greta Bridge *Dur* 3F 19
Gretna *Dum* 2E 11
Gretna Green *Dum* 2E 11
Grewelthorpe *N Yor* 3B 28
Greygarth *N Yor* 3A 28
Grey Green *N Lin* 2D 45
Greysouthen *Cumb* 2B 16
Greystoke *Cumb* 1F 17
Greystoke Gill *Cumb* 2F 17
Greystones *S Yor* 4F 43
Gribthorpe *E Yor* 3D 37
Grimeford Village *Lanc* 1E 41
Grimethorpe *S Yor* 2A 44
Grimoldby *Linc* 4D 47
Grimsargh *Lanc* 3D 33
Grimsby *NE Lin* 2C 46
Grimshaw *Bkbn* 4F 33
Grimshaw Green *Lanc* 1C 40
Grimston *E Yor* 3C 38
Grimston *York* 1C 36
Grindale *E Yor* 3E 31
Grindleford *Derbs* 1E 51
Grindleton *Lanc* 2F 33
Grindley Brook *Shrp* 4D 49
Grindlow *Derbs* 1D 51
Grindon *Nmbd* 2B 4
Grindon *Staf* 3C 50
Gringley on the Hill *Notts* 3D 45
Grinsdale *Cumb* 3E 11
Grinton *N Yor* 1F 27
Gristhorpe *N Yor* 2D 31
Grizebeck *Cumb* 2D 25
Grizedale *Cumb* 1E 25
Grosmont *N Yor* 4B 22
Grove *Notts* 1D 53
Grove, The *Dum* 1A 10
Grovehill *E Yor* 3A 38
Guide *Bkbn* 4F 33
Guide Post *Nmbd* 4E 9
Guilden Sutton *Ches W* 2C 48
Guisborough *Red C* 3F 21
Guiseley *W Yor* 2D 35
Gunby *E Yor* 3D 37
Gunnerside *N Yor* 1E 27
Gunnerton *Nmbd* 1E 13
Gunness *N Lin* 1E 45
Gunsgreenhill *Bord* 1B 4
Gunthorpe *N Lin* 3E 45
Gunthorpe *Notts* 4C 52
Guyzance *Nmbd* 2E 9
Gwernaffield *Flin* 2A 48
Gwernymynydd *Flin* 2A 48
Gwersyllt *Wrex* 3B 48
Gwynfryn *Wrex* 3A 48
Gyfelia *Wrex* 4B 48

H

Habblesthorpe *Notts* 4D 45
Habergham *Lanc* 3A 34
Habrough *NE Lin* 1B 46
Haceby *Linc* 4A 54
Hackenthorpe *S Yor* 4A 44
Hackforth *N Yor* 1B 28
Hackness *N Yor* 1C 30
Hackthorn *Linc* 4F 45
Hackthorpe *Cumb* 2A 18
Hadden *Bord* 3A 4
Haddington *Linc* 2F 53
Hadfield *Derbs* 3C 42
Hadston *Nmbd* 2E 9
Hady *Derbs* 1F 51
Haggate *Lanc* 3A 34
Haggbeck *Cumb* 1F 11
Haggerston *Nmbd* 2C 4
Hagnaby *Linc* 2D 55
Hagworthingham *Linc* 2D 55
Haigh *G Man* 2E 41
Haigh Moor *W Yor* 4E 35
Haighton Green *Lanc* 3D 33
Haile *Cumb* 4B 16
Hainton *Linc* 4B 46
Hainworth *W Yor* 3C 34
Haisthorpe *E Yor* 4E 31
Halam *Notts* 3C 52
Hale *Cumb* 3A 26
Hale *G Man* 4F 41
Hale *Hal* 4C 40
Hale Bank *Hal* 4C 40
Halebarns *G Man* 4F 41
Hales *Staf* 4F 49
Hales Green *Derbs* 4D 51
Halewood *Mers* 4C 40
Halfpenny *Cumb* 2A 26
Halfway *S Yor* 4A 44
Halifax *W Yor* 4C 34
Halkyn *Flin* 1A 48
Hallam Fields *Derbs* 4A 52
Hallands, The *N Lin* 4A 38
Hallbank *Cumb* 1B 26
Hallbankgate *Cumb* 3A 12
Hall Dunnerdale *Cumb* 1D 25
Hallgarth *Dur* 4C 14
Hall Green *Ches E* 3A 50
Hall Green *W Yor* 1F 43
Hall Green *Wrex* 4C 48

Hoole – Langbar

Hoole Ches W 2C 48
Hooley Bridge G Man 1A 42
Hooley Brow G Man 1A 42
Hooton Ches W 1B 48
Hooton Levitt S Yor 3B 44
Hooton Pagnell S Yor 2A 44
Hooton Roberts S Yor 3A 44
Hope Derbs 4D 43
Hope Flin 3B 48
Hope Staf 3D 51
Hopedale Staf 3D 51
Hope Green Ches E 4B 42
Hopetown W Yor 4F 35
Hopperton N Yor 1A 36
Hopton Derbs 3E 51
Horbling Linc 4B 54
Horbury W Yor 1E 43
Horden Dur 4D 15
Horkstow N Lin 1F 45
Hornby Lanc 4A 26
Hornby N Yor 4C 20
(nr Appleton Wiske)
Hornby N Yor 1B 28
(nr Catterick Garrison)
Horncastle Linc 2C 54
Horncliffe Nmbd 2B 4
Horndean Bord 2A 4
Hornsby Cumb 3A 12
Hornsby Gate Cumb 3A 12
Hornsea E Yor 2C 38
Hornsea Burton E Yor 2C 38
Horrocks Fold G Man 1F 41
Horrocksford Lanc 2F 33
Horsehouse N Yor 2F 27
Horseman's Green Wrex 4C 48
Horsforth W Yor 3E 35
Horsington Linc 2B 54
Horsley Derbs 4F 51
Horsley Nmbd 2F 13
(nr Prudhoe)
Horsley Nmbd 3A 8
(nr Rochester)
Horsleyhill Bord 1D 7
Horsleyhope Dur 4F 13
Horsley Woodhouse Derbs 4F 51
Horton Lanc 1A 34
Horton Staf 3B 50
Horton Grange Nmbd 1B 14
Horton Green Ches W 4C 48
Horton in Ribblesdale N Yor 3D 27
Horwich G Man 1E 41
Horwich End Derbs 4C 42
Hoscar Lanc 1C 40
Hotham E Yor 3E 37
Hough Ches E 3F 49
(nr Crewe)
Hough Ches E 1A 50
(nr Wilmslow)
Hougham Linc 4E 53
Hough Green Hal 4C 40
Hough-on-the-Hill Linc 4F 53
Houghton Cumb 3F 11
Houghton Nmbd 2A 14
Houghton Bank Darl 2B 20
Houghton-le-Side Darl 2B 20
Houghton-le-Spring Tyne 3C 14
Houlsyke N Yor 4A 22
Houndwood Bord 1A 4
Hoveringham Notts 4C 52
Hovingham N Yor 3F 29
How Cumb 3A 12
Howden E Yor 4D 37
Howden-le-Wear Dur 1A 20
Howe N Yor 2C 28
Howe, The Cumb 2F 25
Howell Linc 4B 54
Howes Dum 2C 10
Howgill Lanc 2A 34
Howgill N Yor 1C 34
Howick Nmbd 1E 9
Howley Warr 4E 41
Hownam Bord 1F 7
Howsham N Lin 2A 46
Howsham N Yor 4A 30
Howtel Nmbd 3A 4
Hoylake Mers 4A 40
Hoyland S Yor 2F 43
Hoylandswaine S Yor 2E 43
Hubberholme N Yor 3E 27
Hubbert's Bridge Linc 4C 54
Huby N Yor 2E 35
(nr Harrogate)
Huby N Yor 4E 29
(nr York)
Hucknall Notts 4B 52
Huddersfield W Yor 1D 43
Hudswell N Yor 4A 20
Huggate E Yor 1E 37
Hull Hull 4B 38
Hulland Derbs 4E 51
Hulland Moss Derbs 4E 51
Hulland Ward Derbs 4E 51
Hulme G Man 3A 42
Hulme Staf 4B 50
Hulme End Staf 3D 51
Hulme Walfield Ches E 2A 50
Humberside Airport N Lin 1A 46
Humberston NE Lin 2D 47
Humbleton E Yor 3C 38
Humbleton Nmbd 4B 4
Humshaugh Nmbd 1E 13
Huncoat Lanc 3F 33
Hundall Derbs 1F 51
Hunderthwaite Dur 2E 19
Hundleby Linc 2D 55
Hundle Houses Linc 3C 54
Hunger Hill G Man 2E 41
Hunmanby N Yor 3D 31
Hunmanby Sands N Yor 3E 31
Hunsingore N Yor 1A 36
Hunslet W Yor 3F 35
Hunslet Carr W Yor 3F 35
Hunsonby Cumb 1A 18
Hunstanworth Dur 4E 13
Huntington Ches W 2C 48
Huntington York 1C 36
Huntley Staf 4C 50
Hunton N Yor 1A 28
Hunt's Cross Mers 4C 40
Hunwick Dur 1A 20
Hurdsfield Ches E 1B 50
Hurlston Green Lanc 1C 40
Hurst G Man 2B 42
Hurst N Yor 4F 19
Hurst Green Ches E 4D 49
Hurst Green Lanc 3E 33
Hurstwood Lanc 3A 34
Hurworth-on-Tees Darl 3C 20
Hurworth Place Darl 4B 20
Hury Dur 3E 19
Husthwaite N Yor 3E 29
Hut Green N Yor 4B 36
Huthwaite Notts 3A 52
Huttoft Linc 1F 55
Hutton Bord 1B 4
Hutton Cumb 2F 17
Hutton E Yor 1A 38
Hutton Lanc 4C 32
Hutton Bonville N Yor 4C 20
Hutton Buscel N Yor 2C 30
Hutton Conyers N Yor 3C 28
Hutton Cranswick E Yor 1A 38
Hutton End Cumb 1F 17
Hutton Gate Red C 3E 21
Hutton Henry Dur 1D 21
Hutton-le-Hole N Yor 2A 30
Hutton Magna Dur 3A 20
Hutton Mulgrave N Yor 4B 22
Hutton Roof Cumb 3A 26
(nr Kirkby Lonsdale)
Hutton Roof Cumb 1E 17
(nr Penrith)
Hutton Rudby N Yor 4D 21
Huttons Ambo N Yor 4A 30
Hutton Sessay N Yor 3D 29
Hutton Village Red C 3F 21
Hutton Wandesley N Yor 1B 36
Huxley Ches W 2D 49
Huyton Mers 3C 40
Hycemoor Cumb 2B 24
Hyde G Man 3B 42
Hyde Pk. S Yor 2B 44
Hyton Cumb 2B 24

I

Ible Derbs 3E 51
Iburndale N Yor 4B 22
Ickenthwaite Cumb 2E 25
Idle W Yor 3D 35
Idridgehay Derbs 4E 51
Ifton Heath Shrp 4B 48
Ightfield Shrp 4D 49
Ilam Staf 3D 51
Ilderton Nmbd 4C 4
Ilkeston Derbs 4A 52
Ilkley W Yor 2D 35
Illidge Green Ches E 2F 49
Illingworth W Yor 4C 34
Ilton N Yor 3A 28
Immingham NE Lin 1B 46
Immingham Dock NE Lin 1C 46
Ince Ches W 1C 48
Ince Blundell Mers 2B 40
Ince-in-Makerfield G Man 2D 41
Ingbirchworth S Yor 2E 43
Ingham Linc 4F 45
Ingleby Arncliffe N Yor 4D 21
Ingleby Barwick Stoc T 3D 21
Ingleby Greenhow N Yor 4E 21
Inglemire Hull 3A 38
Ingleton Dur 2A 20
Ingleton N Yor 3B 26
Inglewhite Lanc 2D 33
Ingoe Nmbd 1F 13
Ingol Lanc 3D 33
Ingoldmells Linc 2F 55
Ingram Nmbd 1C 8
Ingrow W Yor 3C 34
Ings Cumb 1F 25
Inskip Lanc 3C 32
Ipstones Staf 4C 50
Irby Mers 4A 40
Irby in the Marsh Linc 2E 55
Irby upon Humber NE Lin 2B 46
Ireby Cumb 1D 17
Ireby Lanc 3B 26
Ireleth Cumb 3D 25
Ireshopeburn Dur 1D 19
Ireton Wood Derbs 4E 51
Irlam G Man 3F 41
Ironville Derbs 3A 52
Irthington Cumb 2F 11
Irton N Yor 2D 31
Isabella Pit Nmbd 4F 9
Island Carr N Lin 2F 45
Islesteps Dum 1A 10
Ivegill Cumb 4F 11
Ivelet N Yor 1E 27
Iveston Dur 3A 14

J

Jack Hill N Yor 1D 35
Jacksdale Notts 3A 52
Jamestown Dum 3B 6
Jarrow Tyne 2C 14
Jedburgh Bord 1E 7
Jesmond Tyne 2B 14
Jodrell Bank Ches E 1F 49
Johnby Cumb 1F 17
John O'Gaunts W Yor 4F 35
Johnstown Wrex 4B 48
Jump S Yor 2F 43
Juniper Nmbd 3E 13

K

Kaber Cumb 3C 18
Keadby N Lin 1E 45
Keal Cotes Linc 2D 55
Kearsley G Man 2F 41
Kearstwick Cumb 2B 26
Kearton N Yor 1E 27
Keasden N Yor 4C 26
Keckwick Hal 4D 41
Keddington Linc 4D 47
Keddington Corner Linc 4D 47
Kedleston Derbs 4F 51
Keekle Cumb 3B 16
Keelby Linc 1B 46
Keele Staf 4A 50
Keighley W Yor 2C 34
Keirsleywell Row Nmbd 3C 12
Keisley Cumb 2C 18
Kelbrook Lanc 2B 34
Kelby Linc 4A 54
Keld Cumb 3A 18
Keld N Yor 4D 19
Keldholme N Yor 2A 30
Kelfield N Lin 2E 45
Kelfield N Yor 3B 36
Kelham Notts 3D 53
Kelleth Cumb 4B 18
Kellingley N Yor 4B 36
Kellington N Yor 4B 36
Kelloe Dur 1C 20
Kells Cumb 3A 16
Kelsall Ches W 2D 49
Kelsick Cumb 3C 10
Kelstedge Derbs 2F 51
Kelstern Linc 3C 46
Kelsterton Flin 1A 48
Kelton Dum 1A 10
Kendal Cumb 1A 26
Kendray S Yor 2F 43
Kennythorpe N Yor 4A 30
Kentmere Cumb 4F 17
Kenton Bankfoot Tyne 2B 14
Kentrigg Cumb 1A 26
Kents Bank Cumb 3E 25
Kenyon Warr 3E 41
Kepwick N Yor 1D 29
Kerridge Ches E 1B 50
Kersall Notts 2D 53
Kershopefoot Cumb 4C 6
Keswick Cumb 2D 17
Ketsby Linc 1D 55
Kettleholm Dum 1C 10
Kettleness N Yor 3B 22
Kettleshulme Ches E 1B 50
Kettlesing N Yor 1E 35
Kettlesing Bottom N Yor 1E 35
Kettlethorpe Linc 1E 53
Kettlewell N Yor 3E 27
Kexbrough S Yor 2E 43
Kexby Linc 4E 45
Kexby York 1D 37
Key Green Ches E 2A 50
Key Green N Yor 4B 22
Keyingham E Yor 4C 38
Key's Toft Linc 3E 55
Kibblesworth Tyne 3B 14
Kidburngill Cumb 2B 16
Kidnal Ches W 4C 48
Kidsgrove Staf 3A 50
Kidstones N Yor 2E 27
Kielder Nmbd 3E 7
Kilburn Derbs 4F 51
Kilburn N Yor 3E 29
Kildale N Yor 4F 21
Kildwick N Yor 2C 34
Kilham E Yor 4D 31
Kilham Nmbd 3A 4
Killamarsh Derbs 4A 44
Killerby Darl 3A 20
Killinghall N Yor 1E 35
Killington Cumb 2B 26
Killingworth Tyne 1B 14
Kilnhill Cumb 1D 17
Kilnhurst S Yor 3A 44
Kiln Pit Hill Nmbd 3F 13
Kilnsea E Yor 1E 47
Kilnsey N Yor 4E 27
Kilnwick E Yor 2F 37
Kilpin E Yor 4D 37
Kilpin Pike E Yor 4D 37
Kilton Thorpe Red C 3F 21
Kilvington Notts 4E 53
Kimberley Notts 4A 52
Kimblesworth Dur 4B 14
Kimmerston Nmbd 3B 4
Kingerby Linc 3A 46
Kingholm Quay Dum 1A 10
Kings Clipstone Notts 2C 52
Kingsfold Lanc 4D 33
Kingsforth N Lin 1A 46
Kingsley Ches W 1D 49
Kingsley Staf 4C 50
Kingsley Holt Staf 4C 50
King's Meaburn Cumb 2B 18
Kings Moss Mers 2D 41
King Sterndale Derbs 1C 50
Kingston upon Hull Hull 4B 38 & 58
Kingthorpe Linc 1B 54
Kinkry Hill Cumb 1A 12
Kinninvie Dur 2F 19
Kinsey Heath Ches E 4E 49
Kinsley W Yor 1A 44
Kiplingcotes E Yor 2F 37
Kippax W Yor 3A 36
Kirby Grindalythe N Yor 4C 30
Kirby Hill N Yor 4A 20
(nr Richmond)
Kirby Hill N Yor 4C 28
(nr Ripon)
Kirby Knowle N Yor 2D 29
Kirby Misperton N Yor 3A 30
Kirby Sigston N Yor 1D 29
Kirby Underdale E Yor 1E 37
Kirby Wiske N Yor 2C 28
Kirkandrews-on-Eden Cumb 3E 11
Kirkbampton Cumb 3E 11
Kirkbean Dum 3A 10
Kirk Bramwith S Yor 1C 44
Kirkbride Cumb 3D 11
Kirkbridge N Yor 1B 28
Kirkburn E Yor 1F 37
Kirkburton W Yor 1D 43
Kirkby Linc 3A 46
Kirkby Mers 3C 40
Kirkby N Yor 4E 21
Kirkby Fenside Linc 2D 55
Kirkby Fleetham N Yor 1B 28
Kirkby Green Linc 3A 54
Kirkby-in-Ashfield Notts 3B 52
Kirkby-in-Furness Cumb 2D 25
Kirkby la Thorpe Linc 4B 54
Kirkby Lonsdale Cumb 3B 26
Kirkby Malham N Yor 4D 27
Kirkby Malzeard N Yor 3B 28
Kirkby Mills N Yor 2A 30
Kirkbymoorside N Yor 2F 29
Kirkby on Bain Linc 2C 54
Kirkby Overblow N Yor 2F 35
Kirkby Stephen Cumb 4C 18
Kirkby Thore Cumb 2B 18
Kirkby Wharfe N Yor 2B 36
Kirkcambeck Cumb 2A 12
Kirkconnell Dum 2A 10
Kirkdale Mers 3B 40
Kirk Deighton N Yor 1F 35
Kirk Ella E Yor 4A 38
Kirkgunzeon Dum 2A 10
Kirk Hallam Derbs 4A 52
Kirkham Lanc 3C 32
Kirkham N Yor 4A 30
Kirkhamgate W Yor 4E 35
Kirk Hammerton N Yor 1A 36
Kirkharle Nmbd 4C 8
Kirkheaton Nmbd 1F 13
Kirkheaton W Yor 1D 43
Kirk Ireton Derbs 3E 51
Kirkland Cumb 3B 16
(nr Cleator Moor)
Kirkland Cumb 1B 18
(nr Penrith)
Kirkland Cumb 4D 11
(nr Wigton)
Kirkland Guards Cumb 4C 10
Kirk Langley Derbs 4E 51
Kirkleatham Red C 2E 21
Kirklevington Stoc T 4D 21
Kirklington N Yor 2C 28
Kirklington Notts 3C 52
Kirklinton Cumb 2F 11
Kirk Merrington Dur 1B 20
Kirknewton Nmbd 3B 4
Kirkoswald Cumb 4A 12
Kirkpatrick-Fleming Dum 1D 11
Kirk Sandall S Yor 2C 44
Kirksanton Cumb 2C 24
Kirk Smeaton N Yor 1B 44
Kirkstall W Yor 3E 35
Kirkstile Dum 3B 6
Kirkthorpe W Yor 4F 35
Kirkton Bord 1D 7
Kirkton Dum 1A 10
Kirkwhelpington Nmbd 4B 8
Kirk Yetholm Bord 4A 4
Kirmington N Lin 1B 46
Kirmond le Mire Linc 3B 46
Kirtlebridge Dum 1D 11
Kirtleton Dum 1D 11
Kirton Linc 4D 55
Kirton Notts 2C 52
Kirton End Linc 4C 54
Kirton Holme Linc 4C 54
Kirton in Lindsey N Lin 3F 45
Kiveton Pk. S Yor 4A 44
Knaith Linc 4E 45
Knaith Pk. Linc 4E 45
Knapton York 1B 36
Knaresborough N Yor 1F 35
Knarsdale Nmbd 3B 12
Knayton N Yor 2D 29
Knedlington E Yor 4D 37
Kneesall Notts 2D 53
Kneeton Notts 4D 53
Knenhall Staf 4B 50
Knighton Staf 4F 49
Knitsley Dur 4A 14
Kniveton Derbs 3E 51
Knock Cumb 2B 18
Knolls Green Ches E 1A 50
Knolton Wrex 4B 48
Knott End-on-Sea Lanc 2B 32
Knottingley W Yor 4A 36
Knotts Cumb 2F 17
Knotty Ash Mers 3C 40
Knowefield Cumb 3F 11
Knowesgate Nmbd 4B 8
Knowle Green Lanc 3E 33
Knowsley Mers 3C 40
Knutsford Ches E 1F 49
Knypersley Staf 3A 50
Krumlin W Yor 1C 42

L

Laceby NE Lin 2C 46
Lach Dennis Ches W 1F 49
Lache Ches W 2B 48
Lade Bank Linc 3D 55
Lady Green Mers 2B 40
Lady Hall Cumb 2C 24
Ladykirk Bord 2A 4
Laithes Cumb 1F 17
Laithkirk Dur 2E 19
Lakeside Cumb 2E 25
Lambden Bord 2A 4
Lamberhead Green G Man 2D 41
Lamberton Bord 1B 4
Lambley Nmbd 3B 12
Lambley Notts 4C 52
Lamesley Tyne 3B 14
Lamonby Cumb 1F 17
Lamplugh Cumb 2B 16
Lancaster Lanc 4F 25
Lanchester Dur 4A 14
Land Gate G Man 2D 41
Lane Bottom Lanc 3A 34
Lane Ends Derbs 4E 51
Lane Ends Dur 1A 20
Lane Ends Lanc 1F 33
Laneham Notts 1E 53
Lane Head Dur 3A 20
(nr Hutton Magna)
Lane Head Dur 2F 19
(nr Woodland)
Lane Head G Man 3E 41
Lane Head W Yor 2D 43
Lanehead Dur 4D 13
Lanehead Nmbd 4F 7
Lane Heads Lanc 3C 32
Lanercost Cumb 2A 12
Laneshaw Bridge Lanc 2B 34
Langar Notts 4D 53
Langbar N Yor 1C 34

Langburnshiels – Marshaw

Langburnshiels Bord 2D 7
Langcliffe N Yor 4D 27
Langdale End N Yor 1C 30
Langdon Beck Dur 1D 19
Langford Notts 3E 53
Langho Lanc 3F 33
Langholm Dum 4B 6
Langleeford Nmbd 4B 4
Langley Ches E 1B 50
Langley Derbs 4A 52
Langley Nmbd 2D 13
Langley Common Derbs 4E 51
Langley Green Derbs 4E 51
Langley Moor Dur 4B 14
Langley Pk. Dur 4B 14
Langold Notts 4B 44
Langrick Linc 4C 54
Langrigg Cumb 4C 10
Langsett S Yor 2E 43
Langthorne N Yor 1B 28
Langthorpe N Yor 4C 28
Langthwaite N Yor 4F 19
Langtoft E Yor 4D 31
Langton Dur 3A 20
Langton Linc 2C 54
(nr Horncastle)
Langton Linc 1D 55
(nr Spilsby)
Langton N Yor 4A 30
Langton by Wragby Linc 1B 54
Langwathby Cumb 1A 18
Langwith Derbs 1B 52
Langworth Linc 1A 54
Lanton Bord 1E 7
Lanton Nmbd 3B 4
Larden Green Ches E 3D 49
Lartington Dur 3F 19
Lastingham N Yor 1A 30
Lathom Lanc 2C 40
Laughterton Linc 1E 53
Laughton Linc 3E 45
Laughton Common S Yor 4B 44
Laughton en le Morthen S Yor 4B 44
Laverhay Dum 3A 6
Laversdale Cumb 2F 11
Laverton N Yor 3B 28
Lavister Wrex 3B 48
Lawkland N Yor 4C 26
Laxton E Yor 4D 37
Laxton Notts 2D 53
Laycock W Yor 2C 34
Laytham E Yor 3D 37
Lazenby Red C 3E 21
Lazonby Cumb 1A 18
Lea Derbs 3F 51
Lea Linc 4E 45
Leabrooks Derbs 3A 52
Leadenham Linc 3F 53
Leadgate Cumb 4C 12
Leadgate Dur 3A 14
Leadgate Nmbd 3A 14
Leake N Yor 1D 29
Leake Common Side Linc 3D 55
Leake Fold Hill Linc 3E 55
Leake Hurn's End Linc 4E 55
Lealholm N Yor 4A 22
Leam Derbs 1E 51
Leamside Dur 4C 14
Lease Rigg N Yor 4B 22
Leasgill Cumb 2F 25
Leasingham Linc 4A 54
Leasingthorne Dur 1B 20
Leasowe Mers 3A 40
Leathley N Yor 2E 35
Lea Town Lanc 3C 32
Leavening N Yor 4A 30
Lea Yeat Cumb 2C 26
Leazes Dur 3A 14
Lebberston N Yor 2D 31
Leck Lanc 3B 26
Leconfield E Yor 2A 38
Ledsham Ches W 1B 48
Ledsham W Yor 4A 36
Ledston W Yor 4A 36
Lee Lanc 1D 33
Leece Cumb 4D 25
Leeds W Yor 3E 35 & 59
Leeds Bradford Airport
W Yor 2E 35
Lee Head Derbs 3C 42
Leek Staf 3B 50
Leekbrook Staf 3B 50
Leeming N Yor 2B 28
Leeming Bar N Yor 1B 28
Lee Moor W Yor 4F 35
Lees Derbs 4E 51
Lees G Man 2B 42
Lees W Yor 3C 34
Leeswood Flin 2A 48
Leftwich Ches W 1E 49
Legbourne Linc 4D 47
Legburthwaite Cumb 3E 17
Legsby Linc 4B 46
Leigh G Man 2E 41
Leighton N Yor 3A 28
Leitholm Bord 2A 4
Lelley E Yor 3C 38
Lemington Tyne 2A 14
Lempitlaw Bord 3A 4
Lenacre Cumb 2B 26
Lennel Bord 2A 4
Leppington N Yor 4A 30
Lepton W Yor 1E 43
Lesbury Nmbd 1E 9
Lessonhall Cumb 3D 11
Letwell S Yor 4B 44
Leven E Yor 2B 38
Levens Cumb 2F 25
Levenshulme G Man 3A 42
Leverton Linc 4D 55
Leverton Lucasgate Linc 4E 55
Leverton Outgate Linc 4E 55
Levisham N Yor 1B 30
Leyburn N Yor 1A 28
Leycett Staf 4F 49
Leyland Lanc 4D 33
Leymoor W Yor 1D 43
Lidgett Notts 2C 52
Light Oaks Stoke 3B 50
Lightwood Staf 4C 50
Lightwood Stoke 4B 50
Lightwood Green Ches E 4E 49
Lightwood Green Wrex 4B 48
Lilburn Tower Nmbd 4C 4
Lilliesleaf Bord 1D 7
Limbrick Lanc 1E 41
Limestone Brae Nmbd 4C 12
Linby Notts 3B 52
Lincluden Dum 1A 10
Lincoln Linc 1F 53 & 59
Lindale Cumb 2F 25
Lindal in Furness Cumb 3D 25
Lingdale Red C 3F 21
Lingy Close Cumb 3E 11
Linshiels Nmbd 2A 8
Linstock Cumb 3F 11
Linthwaite W Yor 1D 43
Lintlaw Bord 1A 4
Linton Bord 1F 7
Linton N Yor 4E 27
Linton W Yor 2F 35
Linton Colliery Nmbd 3E 9
Linton-on-Ouse N Yor 4D 29
Lintzford Dur 3A 14
Lintzgarth Dur 4E 13
Linwood Linc 4B 46
Liscard Mers 3B 40
Lissett E Yor 1B 38
Lissington Linc 4B 46
Litherland Mers 3B 40
Littemill Nmbd 1E 9
Little Airmyn N Yor 4D 37
Little Asby Cumb 4B 18
Little Ayton N Yor 3E 21
Little Bampton Cumb 3D 11
Little Barrow Ches W 2C 48
Little Barugh N Yor 3A 30
Little Bavington Nmbd 1E 13
Littlebeck Cumb 3B 18
Little Bispham Bkpl 2B 32
Little Blencow Cumb 1F 17
Little Bollington Ches E 4F 41
Littleborough G Man 1B 42
Littleborough Notts 4E 45
Little Broughton Cumb 1B 16
Little Budworth Ches W 2D 49
Little Burton E Yor 2B 38
Little Carlton Linc 4D 47
Little Carlton Notts 3D 53
Little Catwick E Yor 2B 38
Little Cawthorpe Linc 4D 47
Little Clifton Cumb 2B 16
Little Coates NE Lin 2C 46
Little Crakehall N Yor 1B 28
Little Crosby Mers 2B 40
Little Crosthwaite Cumb 2D 17
Little Cubley Derbs 4D 51
Little Drayton Shrp 4E 49
Little Driffield E Yor 1A 38
Little Eaton Derbs 4F 51
Little Eccleston Lanc 2C 32
Little Fencote N Yor 1B 28
Little Fenton N Yor 3B 36
Little Green Wrex 4C 48
Little Grimsby Linc 3D 47
Little Habton N Yor 3A 30
Little Hale Linc 4B 54
Little Hatfield E Yor 2B 38
Little Hayfield Derbs 4C 42
Little Heck N Yor 4B 36
Little Horton W Yor 3D 35
Little Houghton S Yor 2A 44
Littlehoughton Nmbd 1E 9
Little Hucklow Derbs 1D 51
Little Hulton G Man 2F 41
Little Kelk E Yor 4D 31
Little Langdale Cumb 4E 17
Little Leigh Ches W 1E 49
Little Leven E Yor 2A 38
Little Lever G Man 2F 41
Little Longstone Derbs 1D 51
Littlemoor Derbs 2F 51
Little Mountain Flin 2A 48
Little Musgrave Cumb 3C 18
Little Neston Ches W 1A 48
Little Newsham Dur 3A 20
Little Ormside Cumb 3C 18
Little Orton Cumb 3E 11
Little Ouseburn N Yor 4D 29
Littleover Derb 4F 51
Little Plumpton Lanc 3B 32
Little Ribston N Yor 1F 35
Little Ryle Nmbd 1C 8
Little Salkeld Cumb 1A 18
Little Singleton Lanc 3B 32
Little Smeaton N Yor 1B 44
Little Stainforth N Yor 4D 27
Little Stainton Darl 3C 20
Little Stanney Ches W 1C 48
Little Steeping Linc 2E 55
Little Strickland Cumb 3A 18
Little Sutton Ches W 1B 48
Little Swinburne Nmbd 1E 13
Little Thirkleby N Yor 3D 29
Little Thornton Lanc 2B 32
Little Thorpe W Yor 4D 35
Littlethorpe N Yor 4C 28
Littleton Ches W 2C 48
Little Town Cumb 3D 17
Little Town Lanc 3E 33
Littletown Dur 4C 14
Little Urswick Cumb 3D 25
Little Weighton E Yor 3F 37
Litton Derbs 1D 51
Litton N Yor 3E 27
Liverpool Mers 3B 40 & 60
Liverpool John Lennon Airport
Mers 4C 40
Liversedge W Yor 4D 35
Liverton Red C 3A 22
Liverton Mines Red C 3A 22
Lixwm Flin 1A 48
Llanarmon-yn-Ial Den 3A 48
Llanbedr-Dyffryn-Clwyd Den 3A 48
Llandegla Den 3A 48
Llandynan Den 4A 48
Llanferres Den 2A 48
Llanfynydd Flin 3A 48
Llangollen Den 4A 48
Llan-y-pwll Wrex 3B 48
Llay Wrex 3B 48
Llechrydau Wrex 4A 48
Llong Flin 2A 48
Llwynmawr Wrex 4A 48
Loanend Nmbd 1B 4
Loaningfoot Dum 3A 10
Loansdean Nmbd 4D 9
Locharbriggs Dum 1A 10
Lochfoot Dum 1A 10
Lochmaben Dum 1B 10
Lockerbie Dum 1C 10
Lockhills Cumb 4A 12
Lockington E Yor 2F 37
Lockton N Yor 1B 30
Lofthouse N Yor 3A 28
Lofthouse W Yor 4F 35
Lofthouse Gate W Yor 4F 35
Loftus Red C 3A 22
Loggerheads Den 2A 48
Loggerheads Staf 4F 49
Londesborough E Yor 2E 37
Londonderry N Yor 2C 28
Londonthorpe Linc 4F 53
Long Bennington Linc 4E 53
Longbenton Tyne 2B 14
Longburgh Cumb 3E 11
Longcliffe Derbs 3E 51
Longcroft Cumb 3D 11
Longdale Cumb 4B 18
Longdales Cumb 4A 12
Long Drax N Yor 4C 36
Long Duckmanton Derbs 1A 52
Longford Derbs 4E 51
Longford Shrp 4E 49
Longframlington Nmbd 2D 9
Long Green Ches W 1C 48
Longhirst Nmbd 4E 9
Longhorsley Nmbd 3D 9
Longhoughton Nmbd 1E 9
Longlands Cumb 1D 17
Longlane Derbs 4E 51
Long Lease N Yor 4C 22
Long Marston N Yor 1B 36
Long Marton Cumb 2B 18
Longmoss Ches E 1A 50
Long Newton Stoc T 3C 20
Longnor Staf 2C 50
Longpark Cumb 2F 11
Long Preston N Yor 1A 34
Longridge Lanc 3E 33
Long Riston E Yor 2B 38
Longsdon Staf 3B 50
Longshaw G Man 2D 41
Longshaw Staf 4C 50
Longslow Shrp 4E 49
Longthwaite Cumb 2F 17
Longton Lanc 4C 32
Longton Stoke 4B 50
Longtown Cumb 2E 11
Longwitton Nmbd 4C 8
Lorbottle Nmbd 2C 8
Loscoe Derbs 4A 52
Lostock Gralam Ches W 1E 49
Lostock Green Ches W 1E 49
Lostock Hall Lanc 4D 33
Lostock Junction G Man 2E 41
Lothersdale N Yor 2B 34
Lound Notts 4C 44
Louth Linc 4D 47
Love Clough Lanc 4A 34
Loversall S Yor 3B 44
Low Ackworth W Yor 1A 44
Low Angerton Nmbd 4C 8
Low Barlings Linc 1A 54
Low Bell End N Yor 1A 30
Low Bentham N Yor 4B 26
Low Borrowbridge Cumb 4B 18
Low Bradfield S Yor 3E 43
Low Bradley N Yor 2C 34
Low Braithwaite Cumb 4F 11
Low Brunton Nmbd 1E 13
Low Burnham N Lin 2D 45
Lowca Cumb 2A 16
Low Catton E Yor 1D 37
Low Coniscliffe Darl 3B 20
Low Crosby Cumb 3F 11
Low Dalby N Yor 2B 30
Lowdham Notts 4C 52
Low Dinsdale Darl 3C 20
Low Ellington N Yor 2B 28
Lower Ballam Lanc 3B 32
Lower Crossings Derbs 4C 42
Lower Cumberworth W Yor 2E 43
Lower Darwen Bkbn 4E 33
Lower Dunsforth N Yor 4D 29
Lower Ellastone Staf 4D 51
Lower Hartshay Derbs 3F 51
Lower Hawthwaite Cumb 2D 25
Lower Heysham Lanc 4F 25
Lower Kinnerton Ches W 2B 48
Lower Leigh Staf 4C 50
Lower Mountain Flin 3B 48
Lower Peover Ches W 1F 49
Lower Pilsley Derbs 2A 52
Lower Place G Man 1B 42
Lower Tean Staf 4C 50
Lower Thurnham Lanc 1C 32
Lower Thurvaston Derbs 4E 51
Lower Walton Warr 4E 41
Lower Whitley Ches W 1E 49
Lower Withington Ches E 2A 50
Lower Wych Ches W 4C 48
Loweswater Cumb 2C 16
Low Etherley Dur 2A 20
Low Gate Nmbd 2E 13
Lowgill Cumb 1B 26
Lowgill Lanc 4B 26
Low Grantley N Yor 3B 28
Low Green N Yor 1E 35
Low Hameringham Linc 2D 55
Low Hawsker N Yor 4C 22
Low Hesket Cumb 4F 11
Low Hesleyhurst Nmbd 3C 8
Lowick Cumb 2D 25
Lowick Nmbd 3C 4
Lowick Bridge Cumb 2D 25
Lowick Green Cumb 2D 25
Low Knipe Cumb 2A 18
Low Leighton Derbs 4C 42
Low Lorton Cumb 2C 16
Low Marishes N Yor 3B 30
Low Marnham Notts 2E 53
Low Mill N Yor 1F 29
Low Moor Lanc 2F 33
Low Moor W Yor 4D 35
Low Moorsley Tyne 4C 14
Low Newton-by-the-Sea Nmbd 4E 5
Low Row Cumb 2A 12
(nr Brampton)
Low Row Cumb 4C 10
(nr Wigton)
Low Row N Yor 1E 27
Lowther Cumb 2A 18
Lowthorpe E Yor 4D 31
Lowton G Man 3E 41
Lowton Common G Man 3E 41
Low Toynton Linc 1C 54
Low Westwood Dur 3A 14
Low Whinnow Cumb 3E 11
Low Wood Cumb 2E 25
Low Worsall N Yor 4C 20
Low Wray Cumb 4E 17
Loxley S Yor 4F 43
Lucker Nmbd 3D 5
Ludborough Linc 3C 46
Luddenden W Yor 4C 34
Luddenden Foot W Yor 4C 34
Ludderburn Cumb 1F 25
Luddington N Lin 1E 45
Ludford Linc 4B 46
Ludworth Dur 4C 14
Lumb Lanc 4A 34
Lumby N Yor 3A 36
Lund E Yor 2F 37
Lund N Yor 3C 36
Lunt Mers 2B 40
Lupset W Yor 1F 43
Lupton Cumb 2A 26
Lusby Linc 2D 55
Lydgate G Man 2B 42
Lydgate W Yor 4B 34
Lydiate Mers 2B 40
Lyham Nmbd 3C 4
Lymm Warr 4E 41
Lyneholmeford Cumb 1A 12
Lynemouth Nmbd 3E 9
Lynesack Dur 2F 19
Lytham Lanc 4B 32
Lytham St Anne's Lanc 4B 32
Lythe N Yor 3B 22

M

Mabie Dum 1A 10
Mablethorpe Linc 4F 47
Macclesfield Ches E 1B 50
Macclesfield Forest Ches E 1B 50
Mackworth Derb 4F 51
Madeley Staf 4F 49
Madeley Heath Staf 4F 49
Maer Staf 4F 49
Maes-glas Flin 1A 48
Maeshafn Den 2A 48
Maghull Mers 2B 40
Maiden Law Dur 4A 14
Maidenwell Linc 1D 55
Mainsforth Dur 1C 20
Mainsriddle Dum 3A 10
Makeney Derbs 4F 51
Malcoff Derbs 4C 42
Malham N Yor 4E 27
Malpas Ches W 4C 48
Maltby S Yor 3B 44
Maltby Stoc T 3D 21
Maltby le Marsh Linc 4E 47
Malton N Yor 3A 30
Manby Linc 4D 47
Manchester G Man 3A 42 & 60
Manchester Airport
G Man 4A 42 & 63
Mancot Flin 2B 48
Manfield N Yor 3B 20
Mankinholes W Yor 4B 34
Manley Ches W 1D 49
Manningham W Yor 3D 35
Mansergh Cumb 2B 26
Mansfield Notts 2B 52
Mansfield Woodhouse Notts 2B 52
Mansriggs Cumb 2D 25
Manston W Yor 3F 35
Manthorpe Linc 4F 53
Manton N Lin 2F 45
Manton Notts 1B 52
Maplebeck Notts 2D 53
Mapleton Derbs 4D 51
Mapperley Derbs 4A 52
Mapperley Nott 4B 52
Mapperley Pk. Nott 4B 52
Mappleton E Yor 2C 38
Mapplewell S Yor 2F 43
Marbury Ches E 4D 49
Marchwiel Wrex 4B 48
Mareham le Fen Linc 2C 54
Mareham on the Hill Linc 2C 54
Marehay Derbs 4A 52
Marfleet Hull 4B 38
Marford Wrex 3B 48
Marjoriebanks Dum 1B 10
Markby Linc 1E 55
Markeaton Derb 4F 51
Market Drayton Shrp 4E 49
Market Rasen Linc 4B 46
Market Stainton Linc 4C 46
Market Weighton E Yor 2E 37
Markington N Yor 4B 28
Marley Green Ches E 4D 49
Marley Hill Tyne 3B 14
Marlpool Derbs 4A 52
Marple G Man 4B 42
Marr S Yor 2B 44
Marrick N Yor 1F 27
Marsden Tyne 2C 14
Marsden W Yor 1C 42
Marsett N Yor 2E 27
Marshall Meadows Nmbd 1B 4
Marshaw Lanc 1D 33

Marshchapel – Newlands

Marshchapel *Linc* 3D 47
Marsh Green *Staf* 3A 50
Marsh Lane *Derbs* 1A 52
Marshside *Mers* 1B 40
Marske *N Yor* 4A 20
Marske-by-the-Sea *Red C* 2F 21
Marston *Ches W* 1E 49
Marston *Linc* 4E 53
Marston Montgomery *Derbs* 4D 51
Marthall *Ches E* 1A 50
Marthwaite *Cumb* 1B 26
Martin *Linc* 2C 54
(nr Horncastle)
Martin *Linc* 3B 54
(nr Metheringham)
Martindale *Cumb* 3F 17
Martin Dales *Linc* 2B 54
Martinscroft *Warr* 4E 41
Martin's Moss *Ches E* 2A 50
Marton *Ches E* 2A 50
Marton *Cumb* 3D 25
Marton *E Yor* 4F 31
(nr Bridlington)
Marton *E Yor* 3B 38
(nr Hull)
Marton *Linc* 4E 45
Marton *Midd* 3E 21
Marton *N Yor* 4D 29
(nr Boroughbridge)
Marton *N Yor* 2A 30
(nr Pickering)
Marton Abbey *N Yor* 4E 29
Marton-le-Moor *N Yor* 3C 28
Marylebone *G Man* 2D 41
Maryport *Cumb* 1B 16
Masham *N Yor* 2B 28
Masongill *N Yor* 3B 26
Mastin Moor *Derbs* 1A 52
Matfen *Nmbd* 1F 13
Matlock *Derbs* 3E 51
Matlock Bath *Derbs* 3E 51
Matterdale End *Cumb* 2E 17
Mattersey *Notts* 4C 44
Mattersey Thorpe *Notts* 4C 44
Maulds Meaburn *Cumb* 3B 18
Maunby *N Yor* 2C 28
Mavis Enderby *Linc* 2D 55
Mawbray *Cumb* 4B 10
Mawdesley *Lanc* 1C 40
Maw Green *Ches E* 3F 49
Mawthorpe *Linc* 1E 55
Maxwelltown *Dum* 1A 10
Mayfield *Staf* 4D 51
Meadowbank *Ches W* 2E 49
Meadowfield *Dur* 1B 20
Meadows *Nott* 4B 52
Meaford *Staf* 4A 50
Meal Bank *Cumb* 1A 26
Mealrigg *Cumb* 4C 10
Mealsgate *Cumb* 4D 11
Meanwood *W Yor* 3E 35
Mearbeck *N Yor* 4D 27
Meathop *Cumb* 2F 25
Meaux *E Yor* 3A 38
Medburn *Nmbd* 1A 14
Meden Vale *Notts* 2B 52
Medlam *Linc* 3D 55
Medomsley *Dur* 3A 14
Meerbrook *Staf* 2B 50
Meers Bridge *Linc* 4E 47
Meir *Stoke* 4B 50
Meir Heath *Staf* 4B 50
Melbourne *E Yor* 2D 37
Meldon *Nmbd* 4D 9
Melkington *Nmbd* 2A 4
Melkinthorpe *Cumb* 2A 18
Melkridge *Nmbd* 2C 12
Mellguards *Cumb* 4F 11
Melling *Lanc* 3A 26
Melling *Mers* 2B 40
Melling Mount *Mers* 2C 40
Mellor *G Man* 4B 42
Mellor *Lanc* 3E 33
Mellor Brook *Lanc* 3E 33
Melmerby *Cumb* 1B 18
Melmerby *N Yor* 2F 27
(nr Middleham)
Melmerby *N Yor* 3C 28
(nr Ripon)
Melsonby *N Yor* 4A 20
Meltham *W Yor* 1D 43
Meltham Mills *W Yor* 1D 43
Melton *E Yor* 4F 37
Meltonby *E Yor* 1D 37
Melton Ross *N Lin* 1A 46
Menethorpe *N Yor* 4A 30
Menston *W Yor* 2D 35
Menthorpe *N Yor* 3D 37
Meols *Mers* 3A 40
Mercaston *Derbs* 4E 51
Mere *Ches E* 4F 41
Mere Brow *Lanc* 1C 40
Mereclough *Lanc* 3A 34
Mere Heath *Ches W* 1E 49
Mereside *Bkpl* 3B 32
Merrybent *Darl* 3B 20
Messingham *N Lin* 2E 45
Metheringham *Linc* 2A 54
Methley *W Yor* 4F 35
Methley Junction *W Yor* 4F 35
Mexborough *S Yor* 2A 44
Micklebring *S Yor* 3B 44
Mickleby *N Yor* 3B 22
Micklefield *W Yor* 3A 36
Mickleover *Derb* 4F 51
Micklethwaite *Cumb* 3D 11
Micklethwaite *W Yor* 2D 35
Mickleton *Dur* 2E 19
Mickletown *W Yor* 4F 35
Mickle Trafford *Ches W* 2C 48
Mickley *N Yor* 3B 28
Mickley Square *Nmbd* 2F 13
Middlebie *Dum* 1D 11
Middlecliffe *S Yor* 2A 44
Middleforth Green *Lanc* 4D 33
Middleham *N Yor* 2A 28
Middle Handley *Derbs* 1A 52
Middle Mayfield *Staf* 4D 51
Middle Rainton *Tyne* 4C 14
Middle Rasen *Linc* 4A 46
Middles, The *Dur* 3B 14
Middlesbrough *Midd* 3D 21 & 59
Middlesceugh *Cumb* 4E 11
Middleshaw *Cumb* 2A 26
Middlesmoor *N Yor* 3F 27
Middlestone *Dur* 1B 20
Middlestone Moor *Dur* 1B 20
Middlestown *W Yor* 1E 43
Middleton *Cumb* 2B 26
Middleton *Derbs* 2D 51
(nr Bakewell)
Middleton *Derbs* 3E 51
(nr Wirksworth)
Middleton *G Man* 2A 42
Middleton *Hart* 1E 21
Middleton *Lanc* 1C 32
Middleton *N Yor* 2D 35
(nr Ilkley)
Middleton *N Yor* 2A 30
(nr Pickering)
Middleton *Nmbd* 3D 5
(nr Belford)
Middleton *Nmbd* 4C 8
(nr Morpeth)
Middleton *W Yor* 4E 35
Middleton Green *Staf* 4B 50
Middleton-in-Teesdale *Dur* 2E 19
Middleton One Row *Darl* 3C 20
Middleton-on-Leven *N Yor* 4D 21
Middleton-on-the-Wolds *E Yor* 2F 37
Middleton Quernhow *N Yor* 3C 28
Middleton St George *Darl* 3C 20
Middleton Tyas *N Yor* 4B 20
Middletown *Cumb* 4A 16
Middlewich *Ches E* 2F 49
Middlewood *S Yor* 3F 43
Middridge *Dur* 2B 20
Midge Hall *Lanc* 4D 33
Midgeholme *Cumb* 3B 12
Midgley *W Yor* 4C 34
(nr Halifax)
Midgley *W Yor* 1E 43
(nr Horbury)
Midhopestones *S Yor* 3E 43
Midville *Linc* 3D 55
Milbourne *Nmbd* 1A 14
Milburn *Cumb* 2B 18
Milby *N Yor* 4D 29
Miles Green *Staf* 3A 50
Milfield *Nmbd* 3B 4
Milford *Derbs* 4F 51
Mill Bank *W Yor* 4C 34
Millbeck *Cumb* 2D 17
Millbrook *G Man* 3B 42
Milldale *Staf* 3D 51
Miller's Dale *Derbs* 1D 51
Millers Green *Derbs* 3E 51
Millgate *Lanc* 1A 42
Millhead *Lanc* 3F 25
Mill Hill *Bkbn* 4E 33
Millholme *Cumb* 1A 26
Millhouse *Cumb* 1E 17
Millhousebridge *Dum* 1C 10
Millhouses *S Yor* 4F 43
Millington *E Yor* 1E 37
Millington Green *Derbs* 4E 51
Millom *Cumb* 2C 24
Mill Side *Cumb* 2F 25
Millthorpe *Derbs* 1F 51
Millthrop *Cumb* 1B 26
Milltown *Derbs* 2F 51
Milltown *Dum* 1E 11
Milnrow *G Man* 1B 42
Milnthorpe *Cumb* 2F 25
Milnthorpe *W Yor* 1F 43
Milton *Cumb* 2A 12
(nr Brampton)
Milton *Cumb* 2A 26
(nr Crooklands)
Milton *Dum* 1A 10
Milton *Notts* 1D 53
Milton *Stoke* 3B 50
Milton Green *Ches W* 3C 48
Mindrum *Nmbd* 3A 4
Minera *Wrex* 3A 48
Miningsby *Linc* 2D 55
Minskip *N Yor* 4C 28
Minsteracres *Nmbd* 3F 13
Minting *Linc* 1B 54
Minto *Bord* 1D 7
Mirehouse *Cumb* 3A 16
Mirfield *W Yor* 1E 43
Misson *Notts* 3C 44
Misterton *Notts* 3D 45
Mitford *Nmbd* 4D 9
Mixenden *W Yor* 4C 34
Mixon *Staf* 3C 50
Moat *Cumb* 1F 11
Mobberley *Ches E* 1F 49
Mobberley *Staf* 4C 50
Mockerkin *Cumb* 2B 16
Moddershall *Staf* 4B 50
Mold *Flin* 2A 48
Molescroft *E Yor* 2A 38
Molesden *Nmbd* 4D 9
Mollington *Ches W* 1B 48
Monk Bretton *S Yor* 2F 43
Monk Fryston *N Yor* 4B 36
Monk Hesleden *Dur* 1D 21
Monkhill *Cumb* 3E 11
Monkseaton *Tyne* 1C 14
Monk's Heath *Ches E* 1A 50
Monksthorpe *Linc* 2E 55
Monkwearmouth *Tyne* 3C 14
Monyash *Derbs* 2D 51
Moor Allerton *W Yor* 3E 35
Moorby *Linc* 2C 54
Moore *Hal* 4D 41
Moor End *E Yor* 3E 37
Moorend *Dum* 1D 11
Moorends *S Yor* 1C 44
Moorgate *S Yor* 3A 44
Moorgreen *Notts* 4A 52
Moorhaigh *Notts* 2B 52
Moorhall *Derbs* 1F 51
Moorhouse *Cumb* 3E 11
(nr Carlisle)
Moorhouse *Cumb* 3D 11
(nr Wigton)
Moorhouse *Notts* 2D 53
Moorhouses *Linc* 3C 54
Moor Monkton *N Yor* 1B 36
Moor Row *Cumb* 3B 16
(nr Whitehaven)
Moor Row *Cumb* 4D 11
(nr Wigton)
Moorsholm *Red C* 3F 21
Moorside *G Man* 2B 42
Moortown *Linc* 3A 46
Moortown *W Yor* 3F 35
Mordon *Dur* 2C 20
Morebattle *Bord* 1F 7
Morecambe *Lanc* 4F 25
Moresby Parks *Cumb* 3A 16
Moreton *Mers* 3A 40
Moreton Say *Shrp* 4E 49
Morland *Cumb* 2A 18
Morley *Ches E* 4A 42
Morley *Derbs* 4F 51
Morley *Dur* 2A 20
Morley *W Yor* 4E 35
Morpeth *Nmbd* 4E 9
Morridge Side *Staf* 3C 50
Morridge Top *Staf* 2C 50
Morrington *Dum* 1A 10
Morthen *S Yor* 4A 44
Mortomley *S Yor* 3F 43
Morton *Cumb* 1F 17
(nr Calthwaite)
Morton *Cumb* 3E 11
(nr Carlisle)
Morton *Derbs* 2A 52
Morton *Linc* 3E 45
(nr Gainsborough)
Morton *Linc* 2E 53
(nr Lincoln)
Morton *Notts* 3D 53
Morton-on-Swale *N Yor* 1C 28
Morton Tinmouth *Dur* 2A 20
Morwick *Nmbd* 2E 9
Mosborough *S Yor* 4A 44
Mosedale *Cumb* 1E 17
Moss *S Yor* 1B 44
Moss *Wrex* 3B 48
Moss Bank *Mers* 3D 41
Mossbrow *G Man* 4F 41
Mossburnford *Bord* 1E 7
Mossedge *Cumb* 2F 11
Mossgate *Staf* 4B 50
Moss Lane *Ches E* 1B 50
Mossley *Ches E* 2A 50
Mossley *G Man* 2B 42
Mossley Hill *Mers* 4B 40
Mosspaul *Bord* 3C 6
Moss Side *Cumb* 3C 10
Moss Side *G Man* 3A 42
Moss Side *Lanc* 3B 32
(nr Blackpool)
Moss Side *Lanc* 4D 33
(nr Preston)
Moss Side *Mers* 2B 40
Mosswood *Nmbd* 3F 13
Mossy Lea *Lanc* 1D 41
Moston Green *Ches E* 2F 49
Mostyn *Flin* 4A 40
Mostyn Quay *Flin* 4A 40
Motherby *Cumb* 2F 17
Mottram in Longdendale *G Man* 3B 42
Mottram St Andrew *Ches E* 1A 50
Mouldsworth *Ches W* 1D 49
Moulton *Ches W* 2E 49
Moulton *N Yor* 4B 20
Mountbenger *Bord* 1B 6
Mount Pleasant *Ches E* 3A 50
Mount Pleasant *Derbs* 4F 51
Mouswald *Dum* 1B 10
Mow Cop *Ches E* 3A 50
Mowden *Darl* 3B 20
Mowhaugh *Bord* 4A 4
Much Hoole *Lanc* 4C 32
Mucklestone *Staf* 4F 49
Muckton *Linc* 4D 47
Mugginton *Derbs* 4E 51
Muggintonlane End *Derbs* 4E 51
Muggleswick *Dur* 3F 13
Muker *N Yor* 1E 27
Mumby *Linc* 1F 55
Mungrisdale *Cumb* 1E 17
Murdishaw *Hal* 4D 41
Murton *Cumb* 2C 18
Murton *Dur* 4C 14
Murton *Nmbd* 2B 4
Murton *York* 1C 36
Muscoates *N Yor* 2F 29
Muston *Leics* 4E 53
Muston *N Yor* 3D 31
Myerscough *Lanc* 3C 32
Mynydd Isa *Flin* 2A 48
Mytholmroyd *W Yor* 4C 34
Myton-on-Swale *N Yor* 4D 29

N

Naburn *York* 2B 36
Nab Wood *W Yor* 3D 35
Nafferton *E Yor* 1A 38
Nangreaves *G Man* 1A 42
Nannerch *Flin* 2A 48
Nantwich *Ches E* 3E 49
Nappa *N Yor* 1A 34
Narthwaite *Cumb* 1C 26
Nateby *Cumb* 4C 18
Nateby *Lanc* 2C 32
Natland *Cumb* 2A 26
Navenby *Linc* 3F 53
Nawton *N Yor* 2F 29
Nealhouse *Cumb* 3E 11
Near Sawrey *Cumb* 1E 25
Neasham *Darl* 3C 20
Nedderton *Nmbd* 4E 9
Nelson *Lanc* 3A 34
Nelson Village *Nmbd* 1B 14
Nenthall *Cumb* 4C 12
Nenthead *Cumb* 4C 12
Nercwys *Flin* 2A 48
Nesbit *Nmbd* 3B 4
Nesfield *N Yor* 2C 34
Ness *Ches W* 1B 48
Neston *Ches W* 1A 48
Nether Alderley *Ches E* 1A 50
Nether Burrow *Lanc* 3B 26
Netherby *Cumb* 1E 11
Nether End *Derbs* 1E 51
Netherfield *Notts* 4C 52
Nether Handley *Derbs* 1A 52
Nether Haugh *S Yor* 3A 44
Nether Heage *Derbs* 3F 51
Netherhouses *Cumb* 2D 25
Nether Kellet *Lanc* 4A 26
Nether Langwith *Notts* 1B 52
Nether Moor *Derbs* 2F 51
Nether Padley *Derbs* 1E 51
Nether Poppleton *York* 1B 36
Nether Silton *N Yor* 1D 29
Netherthong *W Yor* 2D 43
Netherton *Cumb* 1B 16
Netherton *Mers* 3B 40
Netherton *Nmbd* 2B 8
Netherton *W Yor* 1D 43
(nr Armitage Bridge)
Netherton *W Yor* 1E 43
(nr Horbury)
Nethertown *Cumb* 4A 16
Nether Wasdale *Cumb* 4C 16
Nether Welton *Cumb* 4E 11
Netherwitton *Nmbd* 3D 9
Nettleham *Linc* 1A 54
Nettlesworth *Dur* 4B 14
Nettleton *Linc* 2B 46
New Abbey *Dum* 2A 10
Newall *W Yor* 2E 35
Newark-on-Trent *Notts* 3D 53
New Balderton *Notts* 3E 53
New Barnetby *N Lin* 1A 46
New Bewick *Nmbd* 4C 4
Newbie *Dum* 2C 10
Newbiggin *Cumb* 2B 18
(nr Appleby)
Newbiggin *Cumb* 4D 25
(nr Barrow-in-Furness)
Newbiggin *Cumb* 4A 12
(nr Cumrew)
Newbiggin *Cumb* 2F 17
(nr Penrith)
Newbiggin *Cumb* 1B 24
(nr Seascale)
Newbiggin *Dur* 4A 14
(nr Consett)
Newbiggin *Dur* 2E 19
(nr Holwick)
Newbiggin *N Yor* 1E 27
(nr Askrigg)
Newbiggin *N Yor* 2E 31
(nr Filey)
Newbiggin *N Yor* 2E 27
(nr Thoralby)
Newbiggin *Nmbd* 4E 13
Newbiggin-by-the-Sea *Nmbd* 4F 9
Newbiggin-on-Lune *Cumb* 4C 18
Newbold *Derbs* 1F 51
New Bolingbroke *Linc* 3D 55
Newbottle *Tyne* 3C 14
New Boultham *Linc* 1F 53
New Brancepeth *Dur* 4B 14
New Bridge *Dum* 1A 10
Newbridge *N Yor* 2B 30
Newbridge *Wrex* 4A 48
New Brighton *Flin* 2A 48
New Brighton *Mers* 3B 40
New Brinsley *Notts* 3A 52
Newbrough *Nmbd* 2D 13
New Broughton *Wrex* 3B 48
Newburgh *Lanc* 1C 40
Newburn *Tyne* 2A 14
Newby *Cumb* 2A 18
Newby *N Yor* 3C 26
(nr Ingleton)
Newby *N Yor* 2D 31
(nr Scarborough)
Newby *N Yor* 3E 21
(nr Stokesley)
Newby Bridge *Cumb* 2E 25
Newby Cote *N Yor* 3C 26
Newby East *Cumb* 3F 11
Newby Head *Cumb* 2A 18
Newby West *Cumb* 3E 11
Newby Wiske *N Yor* 2C 28
Newcastle International Airport *Tyne* 1A 14
Newcastleton *Bord* 4C 6
Newcastle-under-Lyme *Staf* 4A 50
Newcastle upon Tyne *Tyne* 2B 14 & 61
Newchapel *Staf* 3A 50
Newchurch *Lanc* 4A 34
Newchurch in Pendle *Lanc* 3A 34
New Cowper *Cumb* 4C 10
New Crofton *W Yor* 1F 43
New Earswick *York* 1C 36
New Edlington *S Yor* 3B 44
New Ellerby *E Yor* 3B 38
New Ferry *Mers* 4B 40
Newfield *Dur* 3B 14
(nr Chester-le-Street)
Newfield *Dur* 1B 20
(nr Willington)
New Fryston *W Yor* 4A 36
Newhall *Ches E* 4E 49
Newham *Nmbd* 4D 5
New Hartley *Nmbd* 1C 14
Newhaven *Derbs* 2D 51
New Herrington *Tyne* 3C 14
Newhey *G Man* 1B 42
New Holland *N Lin* 4A 38
Newholm *N Yor* 3B 22
New Houghton *Derbs* 2B 52
New Houses *N Yor* 3D 27
New Hutton *Cumb* 1A 26
Newington *Notts* 3C 44
New Inn *N Yor* 3D 27
Newland *Hull* 3A 38
Newland *N Yor* 4C 36
Newlands *Cumb* 1E 17

74 Northern England Regional Atlas

Pickworth – Scamblesby

Pickworth *Linc*. 4A 54
Picton *Ches W* 1C 48
Picton *N Yor* 4D 21
Piercebridge *Darl* 3B 20
Pigdon *Nmbd* 4D 9
Pikehall *Derbs* 3D 51
Pilham *Linc* 3E 45
Pilley *S Yor* 2F 43
Pilling *Lanc* 2C 32
Pilling Lane *Lanc* 2B 32
Pilsbury *Derbs* 2D 51
Pilsley *Derbs* 1E 51
(nr Bakewell)
Pilsley *Derbs* 2A 52
(nr Clay Cross)
Pinfold *Lanc* 1B 40
Pinsley Green *Ches E* 4D 49
Pinxton *Derbs* 3A 52
Pipe Gate *Shrp* 4F 49
Pitsmoor *S Yor* 4F 43
Pittington *Dur* 4C 14
Pity Me *Dur* 4B 14
Place Newton *N Yor* 3B 30
Platt Bridge *G Man* 2E 41
Platt Lane *Shrp* 4D 49
Platts Common *S Yor* 2F 43
Plawsworth *Dur* 4B 14
Pleasington *Bkbn* 4E 33
Pleasley *Derbs* 2B 52
Plenmeller *Nmbd* 2C 12
Plumbland *Cumb* 1C 16
Plumgarths *Cumb* 1F 25
Plumley *Ches E* 1F 49
Plumpton *Cumb* 1F 17
Plumptonfoot *Cumb* 1F 17
Plumpton Head *Cumb* 1A 18
Plungar *Leics* 4D 53
Pockley *N Yor* 2F 29
Pocklington *E Yor* 2E 37
Podmore *Staf* 4F 49
Pole Moor *W Yor* 1C 42
Pollington *E Yor* 1C 44
Polwarth *Bord* 1A 4
Pontblyddyn *Flin* 2A 48
Pontefract *W Yor* 4A 36
Ponteland *Nmbd* 1A 14
Pontfadog *Wrex* 4A 48
Pont-Faen *Shrp* 4A 48
Pont-newydd *Flin* 2A 48
Pontybodkin *Flin* 3A 48
Pool *W Yor* 2E 35
Poole *N Yor* 4A 36
Poolend *Staf* 3B 50
Pooley Bridge *Cumb* 2F 17
Poolfold *Staf* 3A 50
Pool Hey *Lanc* 1B 40
Poolsbrook *Derbs* 1A 52
Port Carlisle *Cumb* 2D 11
Port Clarence *Stoc T* 2D 21
Portington *E Yor* 3D 37
Portinscale *Cumb* 2D 17
Portling *Dum* 3A 10
Port Mulgrave *N Yor* 3A 22
Portobello *W Yor* 1F 43
Portsmouth *W Yor* 4B 34
Port Sunlight *Mers* 4B 40
Potter Brompton *N Yor* 3C 30
Potterhanworth *Linc* 2A 54
Potterhanworth Booths *Linc* 2A 54
Potternewton *W Yor* 3F 35
Potters Brook *Lanc* 1C 32
Potter Somersal *Derbs* 4D 51
Potto *N Yor* 4D 21
Pott Shrigley *Ches E* 1B 50
Poulton-le-Fylde *Lanc* 3B 32
Powburn *Nmbd* 1C 8
Powfoot *Dum* 2C 10
Poynton *Ches E* 4B 42
Prees *Shrp* 4D 49
Preesall *Lanc* 2B 32
Preesall Pk. *Lanc* 2B 32
Prees Higher Heath *Shrp* 4D 49
Prendwick *Nmbd* 1C 8
Prenton *Mers* 4B 40
Prescot *Mers* 3C 40
Pressen *Nmbd* 3A 4
Prestbury *Ches E* 1B 50
Preston *Bord* 1A 4
Preston *E Yor* 3B 38
Preston *Lanc* 4D 33 & 61
Preston *Nmbd* 4D 5
Preston Brook *Hal* 4D 41
Preston-le-Skerne *Dur* 2C 20
Prestonmill *Dum* 3A 10
Preston on the Hill *Hal* 4D 41
Preston-under-Scar *N Yor* 1F 27
Prestwich *G Man* 2A 42
Prestwick *Nmbd* 1A 14
Prestwood *Staf* 4D 51
Priestcliffe *Derbs* 1D 51
Priest Hutton *Lanc* 3A 26
Primrose Hill *Lanc* 2B 40
Primrose Valley *N Yor* 3E 31
Primsidemill *Bord* 4A 4
Prospect *Cumb* 4C 10
Prudhoe *Nmbd* 2F 13
Puddinglake *Ches W* 2F 49
Puddington *Ches W* 1B 48
Pudsey *W Yor* 3E 35
Pulford *Ches W* 3B 48
Purston Jaglin *W Yor* 1A 44
Pyewipe *NE Lin* 1C 46

Q

Quadring Eaudike *Linc* 4C 54
Quaking Houses *Dur* 3A 14
Quarndon *Derbs* 4F 51
Quarrington *Linc* 4A 54
Quarrington Hill *Dur* 1C 20
Quebec *Dur* 4A 14
Queensbury *W Yor* 3D 35
Queensferry *Flin* 2B 48
Queenstown *Bkpl* 3B 32
Quernmore *Lanc* 4A 26
Quixhill *Staf* 4D 51

R

Raby *Cumb* 3C 10
Raby *Mers* 1B 48
Racks *Dum* 1B 10
Radbourne *Derbs* 4E 51
Radcliffe *G Man* 2F 41
Radcliffe *Nmbd* 2E 9
Radcliffe on Trent *Notts* 4C 52
Radford *Nott* 4B 52
Radway Green *Ches E* 3F 49
Ragnall *Notts* 1E 53
Rainford *Mers* 2C 40
Rainford Junction *Mers* 2C 40
Rainhill *Mers* 3C 40
Rainow *Ches E* 1B 50
Rainton *N Yor* 3C 28
Rainworth *Notts* 3B 52
Raisbeck *Cumb* 4B 18
Raise *Cumb* 4C 12
Raithby *Linc* 4D 47
Raithby by Spilsby *Linc* 2D 55
Raithwaite *N Yor* 3B 22
Rakeway *Staf* 4C 50
Rakewood *G Man* 1B 42
Rampside *Cumb* 4D 25
Rampton *Notts* 1D 53
Ramsbottom *G Man* 1F 41
Ramsgill *N Yor* 3A 28
Ramshaw *Dur* 4E 13
Ramshorn *Staf* 4C 50
Ranby *Linc* 1C 54
Ranby *Notts* 4C 44
Rand *Linc* 1B 54
Ranskill *Notts* 4C 44
Rascal Moor *E Yor* 3E 37
Raskelf *N Yor* 3D 29
Rastrick *W Yor* 4D 35
Rathmell *N Yor* 4D 27
Ratten Row *Cumb* 4E 11
Ratten Row *Lanc* 2C 32
Raughton *Cumb* 4E 11
Raughton Head *Cumb* 4E 11
Ravenfield *S Yor* 3A 44
Ravenfield Common *S Yor* 3A 44
Ravenglass *Cumb* 1B 24
Ravenscar *N Yor* 4C 22
Ravenseat *N Yor* 4D 19
Ravenshead *Notts* 3B 52
Ravensmoor *Ches E* 3E 49
Ravensthorpe *W Yor* 4E 35
Ravenstonedale *Cumb* 4C 18
Ravenstown *Cumb* 3E 25
Ravensworth *N Yor* 4A 20
Raw *N Yor* 4C 22
Rawcliffe *E Yor* 4C 36
Rawcliffe *York* 1B 36
Rawcliffe Bridge *E Yor* 4C 36
Rawdon *W Yor* 3E 35
Rawgreen *Nmbd* 3E 13
Rawmarsh *S Yor* 3A 44
Rawson Green *Derbs* 4F 51
Rawtenstall *Lanc* 4A 34
Raylees *Nmbd* 3B 8
Read *Lanc* 3F 33
Reagill *Cumb* 3B 18
Reasby *Linc* 1A 54
Reaseheath *Ches E* 3E 49
Redbourne *N Lin* 2F 45
Redbrook *Wrex* 4D 49
Redburn *Nmbd* 2C 12
Redcar *Red C* 2F 21
Red Dial *Cumb* 4D 11
Reddish *G Man* 3A 42
Redesdale Camp *Nmbd* 3A 8
Redesmouth *Nmbd* 4A 8
Redford *Dur* 1F 19
Redfordgreen *Bord* 1B 6
Red Hill *W Yor* 4A 36
Redmain *Cumb* 1C 16
Redmarshall *Stoc T* 2C 20
Redmile *Leics* 4D 53
Redmire *N Yor* 1F 27
Red Rock *G Man* 2D 41
Red Row *Nmbd* 3E 9
Red Street *Staf* 3A 50
Redvales *G Man* 2A 42
Redworth *Darl* 2B 20
Reedham *Linc* 3C 54
Reedness *E Yor* 4E 37
Reeds Beck *Linc* 2C 54
Reepham *Linc* 1A 54
Reeth *N Yor* 1F 27
Reighton *N Yor* 3E 31
Renishaw *Derbs* 1A 52
Rennington *Nmbd* 1E 9
Renwick *Cumb* 4A 12
Reston *Bord* 1A 4
Retford *Notts* 4D 45
Revesby *Linc* 2C 54
Rhewl *Den* 4A 48
Rhewl *Shrp* 4B 48
Rhewl-Mostyn *Flin* 4A 40
Rhiwabon *Wrex* 4B 48
Rhodes *G Man* 2A 42
Rhodesia *Notts* 4B 44
Rhosesmor *Flin* 2A 48
Rhosllanerchrugog *Wrex* 4A 48
Rhostyllen *Wrex* 4B 48
Rhoswiel *Shrp* 4A 48
Rhuddall Heath *Ches W* 2D 49
Rhydtalog *Flin* 3A 48
Rhydymwyn *Flin* 2A 48
Ribbleton *Lanc* 3D 33
Ribby *Lanc* 3C 32
Ribchester *Lanc* 3E 33
Riber *Derbs* 3F 51
Riby *Linc* 2B 46
Riccall *N Yor* 3C 36
Richmond *N Yor* 4A 20
Rickerby *Cumb* 3F 11
Rickleton *Tyne* 3B 14
Riddings *Derbs* 3A 52
Riddlesden *W Yor* 2C 34
Ridgeway *Derbs* 3F 51
(nr Alfreton)
Ridgeway *Derbs* 4A 44
(nr Sheffield)
Ridgeway *Staf* 3A 50
Ridgeway Moor *Derbs* 4A 44
Ridgwardine *Shrp* 4E 49
Riding Mill *Nmbd* 2F 13
Ridley *Nmbd* 2C 12
Ridsdale *Nmbd* 4B 8
Rievaulx *N Yor* 2E 29
Rift House *Hart* 1D 21
Rigg *Dum* 2D 11
Rigsby *Linc* 1E 55
Riley Green *Lanc* 4E 33
Rillington *N Yor* 3B 30
Rimington *Lanc* 2A 34
Rimswell *E Yor* 4D 39
Ringinglow *S Yor* 4E 43
Ring o' Bells *Lanc* 1C 40
Ripley *Derbs* 3A 52
Ripley *N Yor* 4B 28
Riplingham *E Yor* 3F 37
Ripon *N Yor* 3C 28
Ripponden *W Yor* 1C 42
Risby *E Yor* 3A 38
Risby *N Lin* 1F 45
Rise *E Yor* 2B 38
Rise End *Derbs* 3E 51
Riseholme *Linc* 1F 53
Rishton *Lanc* 3F 33
Rishworth *W Yor* 1C 42
Risley *Derbs* 4A 52
Risley *Warr* 3E 41
Risplith *N Yor* 4B 28
Rivington *Lanc* 1E 41
Roach Bridge *Lanc* 4D 33
Roadhead *Cumb* 1A 12
Roa Island *Cumb* 4D 25
Roberton *Bord* 1C 6
Roberttown *W Yor* 4D 35
Robin Hood *Lanc* 1D 41
Robin Hood *W Yor* 4F 35
Robin Hood's Bay *N Yor* 4C 22
Roby Mill *Lanc* 2D 41
Rocester *Staf* 4D 51
Rochdale *G Man* 1A 42
Rochester *Nmbd* 3A 8
Rock *Nmbd* 4E 5
Rockcliffe *Cumb* 2E 11
Rockcliffe *Dum* 3A 10
Rockcliffe Cross *Cumb* 2E 11
Rock Ferry *Mers* 4B 40
Roddam *Nmbd* 4C 4
Roddymoor *Dur* 1A 20
Rode Heath *Ches E* 3A 50
Rodeheath *Ches E* 2A 50
Rodsley *Derbs* 4E 51
Roecliffe *N Yor* 4C 28
Roger Ground *Cumb* 1E 25
Roker *Tyne* 3D 15
Rolleston *Notts* 3D 53
Rolston *E Yor* 2C 38
Romaldkirk *Dur* 2E 19
Romanby *N Yor* 1C 28
Romiley *G Man* 3B 42
Rookby *Cumb* 3D 19
Rookhope *Dur* 4E 13
Rooking *Cumb* 3F 17
Roos *E Yor* 3C 38
Roosebeck *Cumb* 4D 25
Roosecote *Cumb* 4D 25
Ropsley *Linc* 4F 53
Roseacre *Lanc* 3C 32
Rosedale Abbey *N Yor* 1A 30
Roseden *Nmbd* 4C 4
Rose Hill *Lanc* 3A 34
Roseworth *Stoc T* 2D 21
Rosgill *Cumb* 3A 18
Rosley *Cumb* 4E 11
Ross *Bord* 1B 4
Ross *Nmbd* 3D 5
Rossett *Wrex* 3B 48
Rossington *S Yor* 3C 44
Rostherne *Ches E* 4F 41
Rostholme *S Yor* 2B 44
Rosthwaite *Cumb* 3D 17
Roston *Derbs* 4D 51
Rothbury *Nmbd* 2C 8
Rotherham *S Yor* 3A 44
Rothley *Nmbd* 4C 8
Rothwell *Linc* 3B 46
Rothwell *W Yor* 4F 35
Rotsea *E Yor* 1A 38
Rottington *Cumb* 3A 16
Rough Close *Staf* 4B 50
Roughcote *Staf* 4B 50
Roughlee *Lanc* 2A 34
Roughsike *Cumb* 1A 12
Roughton *Linc* 2C 54
Roundhay *W Yor* 3F 35
Roundthwaite *Cumb* 4B 18
Routh *E Yor* 2A 38
Row *Cumb* 2F 25
(nr Kendal)
Row *Cumb* 1B 18
(nr Penrith)
Row, The *Lanc* 3F 25
Rowanburn *Dum* 1F 11
Rowarth *Derbs* 4C 42
Rowfoot *Nmbd* 2B 12
Rowland *Derbs* 1E 51
Rowlands Gill *Tyne* 3A 14
Rowley *Dur* 4F 13
Rowley *E Yor* 3F 37
Rowley Hill *W Yor* 1D 43
Rowrah *Cumb* 3B 16
Rowsley *Derbs* 2E 51
Rowston *Linc* 3A 54
Rowthorne *Derbs* 2A 52
Rowton *Ches W* 2C 48
Roxby *N Lin* 1F 45
Roxby *N Yor* 3A 22
Royal Oak *Darl* 2B 20
Royal Oak *Lanc* 2C 40
Royal Oak *N Yor* 3E 31
Royal's Green *Ches E* 4E 49
Royston *S Yor* 1F 43
Royton *G Man* 2B 42
Ruabon *Wrex* 4B 48
Ruckcroft *Cumb* 4A 12
Ruckland *Linc* 1D 55
Rudby *N Yor* 4D 21
Rudheath *Ches W* 1E 49
Rudston *E Yor* 4D 31
Rudyard *Staf* 3B 50
Rufford *Lanc* 1C 40
Rufforth *York* 1B 36
Runcorn *Hal* 4D 41
Runshaw Moor *Lanc* 1D 41
Runswick Bay *N Yor* 3B 22
Rusholme *G Man* 3A 42
Rushton *Ches W* 2D 49
Rushton Spencer *Staf* 2B 50
Rushyford *Dur* 2B 20
Ruskington *Linc* 3A 54
Rusland *Cumb* 2E 25
Ruston *N Yor* 2C 30
Ruston Parva *E Yor* 4D 31
Ruswarp *N Yor* 4B 22
Ruthwaite *Cumb* 1D 17
Ruthwell *Dum* 2C 10
Ryal *Nmbd* 1F 13
Rydal *Cumb* 4E 17
Ryecroft Gate *Staf* 2B 50
Ryehill *E Yor* 4C 38
Ryhill *W Yor* 1F 43
Ryhope *Tyne* 3D 15
Ryhope Colliery *Tyne* 3D 15
Rylands *Notts* 4B 52
Rylstone *N Yor* 1B 34
Ryther *N Yor* 3B 36
Ryton *N Yor* 3A 30
Ryton *Tyne* 2A 14
Ryton Woodside *Tyne* 2A 14

S

Sabden *Lanc* 3F 33
Sacriston *Dur* 4B 14
Sadberge *Darl* 3C 20
Sadgill *Cumb* 4F 17
Saighton *Ches W* 2C 48
St Anne's *Lanc* 4B 32
St Bees *Cumb* 3A 16
St Helen Auckland *Dur* 2A 20
St Helens *Cumb* 1B 16
St Helens *Mers* 3D 41
St John's Chapel *Dur* 1D 19
St Martin's *Shrp* 4B 48
St Michael's on Wyre *Lanc* 2C 32
Sale *G Man* 3F 41
Saleby *Linc* 1E 55
Salesbury *Lanc* 3E 33
Salford *G Man* 3A 42
Salkeld Dykes *Cumb* 1A 18
Salmonby *Linc* 1D 55
Salta *Cumb* 4B 10
Saltaire *W Yor* 3D 35
Saltburn-by-the-Sea *Red C* 2F 21
Saltcoats *Cumb* 1B 24
Salt End *E Yor* 4B 38
Salter *Lanc* 4B 26
Salterforth *Lanc* 2A 34
Salterswall *Ches W* 2E 49
Saltfleet *Linc* 3E 47
Saltfleetby All Saints *Linc* 3E 47
Saltfleetby St Clement *Linc* 3E 47
Saltfleetby St Peter *Linc* 4E 47
Saltmarshe *E Yor* 4D 37
Saltney *Flin* 2B 48
Salton *N Yor* 3A 30
Saltwick *Nmbd* 1A 14
Samlesbury *Lanc* 3D 33
Samlesbury Bottoms *Lanc* 4E 33
Sancton *E Yor* 3F 37
Sandale *Cumb* 4D 11
Sandal Magna *W Yor* 1F 43
Sandbach *Ches E* 2F 49
Sandford *Cumb* 3C 18
Sandford *Shrp* 4D 49
Sandhoe *Nmbd* 2E 13
Sand Hole *E Yor* 3E 37
Sandholme *E Yor* 3E 37
Sandholme *Linc* 4D 55
Sand Hutton *N Yor* 1C 36
Sandhutton *N Yor* 2C 28
Sandiacre *Derbs* 4A 52
Sandilands *Linc* 4F 47
Sandiway *Ches W* 1E 49
Sandlow Green *Ches E* 2F 49
Sandsend *N Yor* 3B 22
Sandside *Cumb* 3E 25
Sandtoft *N Lin* 2D 45
Sandwick *Cumb* 3F 17
Sandwith *Cumb* 3A 16
Sandy Bank *Linc* 3C 54
Sandycroft *Flin* 2B 48
Sandyhills *Dum* 3A 10
Sandylands *Lanc* 4F 25
Santon *Cumb* 4B 16
Santon Bridge *Cumb* 4C 16
Sapperton *Derbs* 4D 51
Sapperton *Linc* 4A 54
Satley *Dur* 4A 14
Satron *N Yor* 1E 27
Satterthwaite *Cumb* 1E 25
Saughall *Ches W* 1B 48
Saughtree *Bord* 3D 7
Saundby *Notts* 4D 45
Sausthorpe *Linc* 2D 55
Saverley Green *Staf* 4B 50
Sawdon *N Yor* 2C 30
Sawley *Lanc* 2F 33
Sawley *N Yor* 4B 28
Saxby *Linc* 4A 46
Saxby All Saints *N Lin* 1F 45
Saxilby *Linc* 1E 53
Saxondale *Notts* 4C 52
Saxton *N Yor* 3A 36
Scackleton *N Yor* 3F 29
Scaftworth *Notts* 3C 44
Scagglethorpe *N Yor* 3B 30
Scaitcliffe *Lanc* 4F 33
Scalby *E Yor* 4E 37
Scalby *N Yor* 1D 31
Scalby Mills *N Yor* 1D 31
Scaleby *Cumb* 2F 11
Scalebyhill *Cumb* 2F 11
Scale Houses *Cumb* 4A 12
Scales *Cumb* 3D 25
(nr Barrow-in-Furness)
Scales *Cumb* 2E 17
(nr Keswick)
Scaling *N Yor* 3A 22
Scaling Dam *Red C* 3A 22
Scamblesby *Linc* 1C 54

Published by Geographers' A-Z Map Company Limited
An imprint of HarperCollins Publishers
Westerhill Road
Bishopbriggs
Glasgow
G64 2QT

HarperCollinsPublishers
1st Floor, Watermarque Building, Ringsend Road, Dublin 4, Ireland

www.az.co.uk
a-z.maps@harpercollins.co.uk

5th edition 2022

© Collins Bartholomew Ltd 2022

This product uses map data licenced from Ordnance Survey
© Crown copyright and database rights 2022 OS 100018598

AZ, A-Z and AtoZ are registered trademarks of Geographers' A-Z Map Company Limited

A catalogue record for this book is available from the British Library.

ISBN 978-0-00-853219-2

10 9 8 7 6 5 4 3 2 1

Printed in the UK

MIX
Paper from
responsible sources
FSC™ C007454

www.fsc.org